Praise for *Alive Until You're Dead*

"Reading this book is like finding a friend, someone who is a bit wiser and more clear-sighted, honest and plainspoken, someone who faces her fears and will help you face yours. *Alive Until You're Dead* should be required reading for all mortals."

— RUTH OZEKI, author of *The Book of Form and Emptiness*

"Deep, delightful, challenging, uplifting, this wonderful book is full of wisdom and a must-read for all of us."

— JOAN HALIFAX, author of *Being with Dying* and *Standing at the Edge*

"I truly love anything Susan Moon writes. These latest essays are filled with her trademark simple-but-profound life stories and humor woven with Buddhist teachings and oodles of wisdom. Her depth and authenticity, as always, shine through. I can think of no better guide along the path to aging and the unknown than Susan Moon."

— DIANA WINSTON, director of mindfulness education at UCLA's Mindful Awareness Research Center, author of *The Little Book of Being*

"In this wonderful book Susan Moon uses stories of her life to explore the joys and tragedies of being human. She is a great satirist, and this book is full of humor and wisdom."

— WES NISKER, author of *The Essential Crazy Wisdom* and *Buddha's Nature*

"As she faces the inevitable end of her long life, Susan Moon considers what it means to be satisfied. With wit and the wisdom of decades of Buddhist practice, Moon considers the gifts and struggles of age, where joy and sorrow walk hand in hand."

— SALLIE TISDALE, author of *The Lie About the Truck* and *Advice for Future Corpses*

Alive Until You're Dead

NOTES ON THE HOME STRETCH

SUSAN MOON

SHAMBHALA

Shambhala Publications, Inc.
2129 13th Street
Boulder, Colorado 80302
www.shambhala.com

Cover art: FoxyImage/Shutterstock.com | Cover and interior design: Kate E. White
Photo on page xiv by Jeannie O'Connor | Author photo on back cover and
page 205 by Vickie Leonard | Photo on page 206 by Sandy de Lissovoy

9 8 7 6 5 4 3 2 1

First Edition
Printed in the United States of America

⊗ This edition is printed on acid-free paper that meets the
American National Standards Institute Z39.48 Standard.
♻ Shambhala Publications makes every effort to print on recycled
paper. For more information please visit www.shambhala.com.
Shambhala Publications is distributed worldwide by
Penguin Random House, Inc., and its subsidiaries.

LIBRARY OF CONGRESS CATALOGING-IN-PUBLICATION DATA
Names: Moon, Susan, 1942– author.
Title: Alive until you're dead: notes on the home stretch / Susan Moon.
Description: Boulder: Shambhala, 2022.
Identifiers: LCCN 2021038865 | ISBN 9781611809633 (trade paperback)
Subjects: LCSH: Aging–Religious aspects–Buddhism. | Death–
Religious aspects–Buddhism.
Classification: LCC BQ5435 .M66 2022 | DDC 294.3/423–dc23
LC record available at https://lccn.loc.gov/2021038865

for Noah and Sandy
no longer young, not yet old,
working, loving, raising children,
somewhere in the middle of birth-and-death

Contents

Introduction

You don't know how long you're going to live. You know you're going to die, but it doesn't seem real. Then, as you get older, people you love die. You ache for them. Your mortality impresses itself upon you. You notice the impermanence of all living things, maybe even of the human species, and you realize how amazing it is to be alive. You notice the joy of feeling connected to something beyond yourself. You catch a glimpse of what Zen Master Dogen meant when he said nine hundred years ago, "The entire universe is the true human body."

I'm not nearly as worried about getting old as I used to be, because worrying is what you do about something that hasn't happened yet, and I already *am* old, with a history of getting old behind me. I've already gotten my titanium knees and my silicone lens implants, and now, in defiance of nature, I can walk and see better than I could when I was ten years younger. The rest of me, however, the organic part, has not improved in the last decade, and the general downward trend is likely to continue. I see now that doing battle against aging is not a good use of my time and so letting go of that fight is a big relief. I have a wider view, and it's not because of my lens implants. Although there are fewer and fewer moments left in front of me, and the days flip by faster than ever, something strange is happening. Each moment, when I come to it, has more time in it than the moments of years gone by.

One day when I was about eight, I persuaded my best friend that it would be fun to get lost on purpose, to see what it feels like to be lost. I was curious. Children were always getting lost in books and fairy tales and entering enchanted territory. I wanted to make a border crossing, too. My friend agreed. In those days, my parents let me have the run of the neighborhood—a quiet residential part of town where I knew the neighbors and they knew me. So we told my parents we were going out to play and we slipped away. It was a sunny morning and the streets were quiet, with hardly any cars. We walked to the end of my block, turned, zigzagged, circled, taking unfamiliar streets, lanes, alleys, deliberately not looking back, not keeping track, though I was aware that we were mostly going down. In one spot, broken bundles of shiny election flyers were strewn on the sidewalk and we pocketed some, thinking they might be special. We passed from a neighborhood of single-family houses into a neighborhood of duplexes and triplexes. We were together, and we were excited. After a while we stopped and looked around, and we didn't know which way was home. We had accomplished our mission—we were lost! I felt a rush of adrenaline that sharpened my senses. I smelled the toasty smell of dry maple leaves in the gutter. I saw how the sky wheeled above us, between the unfamiliar roofs on either side of the street. I was lost, but there I was! Really there, in that place.

We were explorers, just the right amount scared or maybe a little beyond just right. We followed our noses and headed uphill. It began to feel like a long time that we'd been gone, and our thoughts turned to our parents. Would they have noticed we were gone? We walked and walked and came at last to a street I recognized; after that we found our way easily. As we approached my house, we saw on the front porch all four of our parents, standing shoulder to shoulder, peering out. They were worried, they were mad, they had called the police. My parents told me I must never ever again go off like that without telling them. As punishment, I wasn't allowed to go to the dog show in Madison Square Garden that afternoon with the rest of the family.

Getting lost on purpose seems like a strange way to try to find yourself, but I think that's what an explorer does. I'm a seeking old person, as I was a seeking child (now I sometimes get lost without even trying) and I report on my explorations here. These essays are about my ongoing discovery that I am alive. Though I make references to Zen, you certainly don't have to be a Buddhist to read this book. Many of my dearest friends and relatives are not Buddhists. I was a human being long before I was a Buddhist, and I'm still more human than Buddhist. I'm curious by nature, and all my life I've been wondering, *What does it mean to be a human being?* Now I ask, *What does it mean to be an old human who is going to die? What's the point of life if you're going to die anyway?*

The question sounds dreary, but it's not. It's a question born of a bright curiosity. I've always been curious about this world, about how a spider can spin from its own body the very thread it hangs by, or what it would be like to live in a house on stilts. I've learned to be curious about difficult things, too. Years ago, when I was in a period of acute anxiety, a therapist asked me, "Can you get curious about this?" That's a good mantra. I now take it with me through thick and thin: *Can I get curious about this?*

When I was a young adult, my travels were geographical. I liked to make border crossings into unfamiliar territory, to connect with people on the other side, and to find out over and over that there wasn't any other side. I saw wonderfully different ways of being human and I saw that they weren't oppositional.

When I was sixteen, I went to a Quaker work camp for teenagers on an Indian reservation in North Dakota, and under the supervision of Mandan elders, we helped to build a traditional earth lodge. I spent a college summer doing a volunteer job in Johannesburg, South Africa, hosted by a courageous white couple working against apartheid. The following summer I went to Mississippi, along with other volunteers from the North, to take part in the civil rights movement of Black Americans. On these journeys I gained much more than I gave, and these experiences enlarged my understanding of what it means to be a human being.

I married, had two children, got divorced, and was a single mother for many years. The kids had a steadying effect on me, though I wish I had been steadier still for their sakes. My explorations into being human continued, and sometimes we went adventuring together. We camped by a lake in the High Sierra, spooning instant oatmeal out of our Sierra cups, watching the sun paint the rock face gold. My children gave immeasurable meaning to my life, waking me up to love over and over, giving me chance after chance. They stopped short of giving me the final answer to the question of what it means to be a human being, because that wasn't their job. I needed that question to keep me on the path.

My wondering took me to Zen practice more than forty years ago, when my children were still small. Zen was the next thing, after my children, that called on me to settle and focus. Zen practice told me to sit down and stay still. Zen practice encouraged me to journey within. To quote Dogen (again), "Why leave behind your proper place, which exists right in your own home, and wander aimlessly off to the dusty realms of other lands? The Great Way lies directly before you. . . . You have gained the pivotal opportunity of human form. Do not let your time pass in vain." I got the idea, but my wanderlust wasn't completely extinguished. I love my home temple and my home sangha, but I have also attended or led retreats in many different places, journeying within and without at the same time.

It's old age, even more than motherhood or Zen practice, that has made the idea of traveling to the dusty realms of other lands less appealing. And most recently, the long sheltering in place during the pandemic has had the unexpected personal benefit of showing me how peaceful it can be to stay home. I'm still exploring. I'm becoming an armchair traveler like my grandparents, who had been avid voyagers in their youth and who, in their old age, preferred to sit in comfy chairs and look at slides of India rather than go there. From right here inside my head, on my cushion or in my chair, in my household, in my own neighborhood, with a little help from technology, I travel to distant places and times. As I come closer to the end of my life, my small self expands to join with other beings in one big being.

With this collection of essays, I want to share with you my explorations about "the pivotal opportunity of human form." I give you not a catalog of aches and pains but field notes from my research: What does it mean to be a human being approaching death?

I'm the main subject of the study, along with anecdotal evidence from people I know, so it's qualitative research, but I hope it has meaning for you. I offer a few observations: The nearer I get to death, the more alive I feel. The more I consider my own mortality, the less afraid I am of dying. And the older I get, the more readily I can put myself aside. I see the unselfishness in other old people, and I trust it's growing in me, too. Their examples help me move in that direction.

In the Zen tradition, a wooden board is struck with a mallet to call the monks to meditation. The board is called the *han*, and the verse that's written on the han says, "Great is the matter of birth and death. All is impermanent, quickly passing. Wake up! Wake up, each one! Don't waste this life."

This doesn't mean you have to hurry. You can take the pace that's right for you. You don't have to run to wake up where you already are.

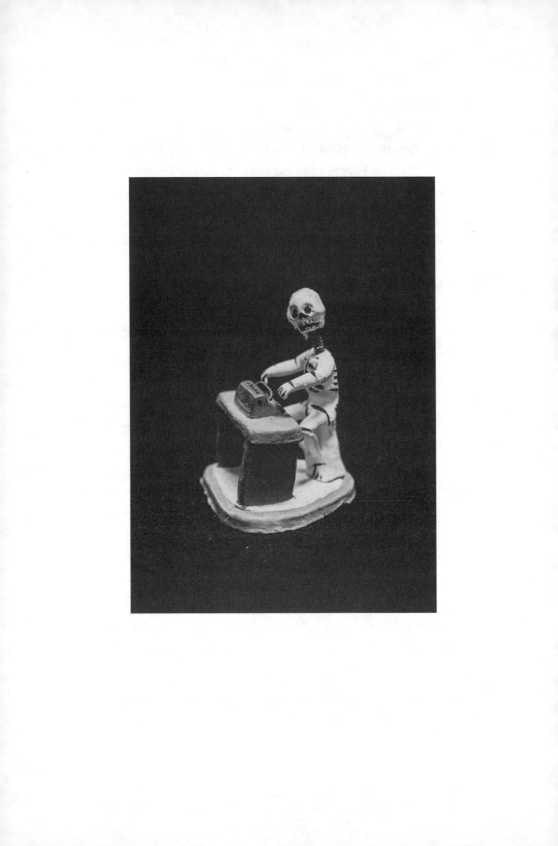

Alive Until
You're Dead

Joyful Effort

W HEN MY SON Sandy was five, he was a big *Star Wars* fan. For a while, he drew many pictures of lightsabers, and the exhortation "May the Force be with you!" was often heard around our house. One day Sandy told me, "When you love somebody, you can feel the love coming straight out of your heart in a line, like a lightsaber, and it touches the other person." This image cheers me still.

In Buddhist teaching, a bodhisattva is one who lives to free all beings from suffering–a tall order indeed. But as long as you wish to ease someone else's pain now and again, you've got at least one foot on the bodhisattva path. And you don't have to be a Buddhist to be a bodhisattva.

Buddhist teachings list various virtues you can cultivate to help you free beings from suffering. My current favorite, the one I'm working on at the moment, is joyful effort, or *virya* in Sanskrit. It's a good quality to cultivate at any age, and especially good for someone who has reached the age when you meet a lot of jars you can't open. You can still have virya even if you can't get at the apricot jam. Virya is not about muscle power. Virya doesn't care about age. I'm not too old to make an effort, nor too old to feel joy. I put the effort and the joy together and I've got my joyful effort.

I think of virya as a kind of life force, like chi in Chinese medicine. It's vitality itself, the very thing a corpse is lacking. It comes out of us toward other people and everything around us and connects us. It's what Sandy was talking about: virya, the lightsaber of love.

Where does the joy in joyful effort come from? When I let go of restraint and give myself away to the activity of helping somebody else, it feels good. But there's an old habit of mind that hesitates: *Wait, wait! Do I have enough time for this? Do I have enough strength for this?* I'm not talking due diligence here; I'm talking balking. When I can let go of those questions and just do it, whatever it is, that's a great relief. I go beyond myself.

I learned about virya from my father as well as my son. I learned that this lightsaber can pass through obstacles. My parents divorced late in life, when they were about sixty, and my father married again. He was a vigorous, athletic person, but he went blind from detached retinas shortly after he remarried.

Like a baby born into a brand-new world, he had to learn everything from scratch. Unlike a baby, he was born into this new life both old and blind. If you've been a sighted person all your life, you have to learn all over again how to do the most basic things, like pouring yourself a cup of tea. I remember watching him hold the kettle of hot water in one hand and the cup in the other. He crooked one finger over the rim of the cup as he poured, so that he could feel when the hot water was getting close to the top. This beginning again took perseverance and courage, and my father had both.

With his second wife, who was much younger than he, my father had two children he literally never saw, though he was extremely attentive to them. He became ill with cancer after the second child was born, and they were only seven and ten when he died. They are adults now, and their mother is still healthy and loving, as she has been from the beginning. Their father, however, was not only old but blind and struggling with bone-aching cancer, and in spite of all this, he was a devoted father.

I watched him get down on his hands and knees and join the kids in playing with the farm set, moving the little wooden animals around, seeing them with his fingers, making the cows go *moo* and the pigs go *oink*. Sometimes I saw his face flinch with pain, but that didn't stop him from helping the kids put the cows back in the barn for milking.

How did he come by this joyful energy in the last stage of his life—sick, blind, and frail as he was? It must have been the energy of love. Where else could he have gotten it?

Virya is translated in many other ways besides "joyful effort," including "zeal," "enthusiastic energy," "vigor," "right endeavor," "perseverance," and even "courage." I knew there were many facets to this word, and a Sanskrit-scholar friend recently told me of another: the word *virya* originally meant not only "vigor" but also "semen." Oh no! The Latin word *vir*, meaning "man," comes from that root, as does the English word *virility*, so it's a highly gendered word. Let's un-gender virya; let's claim it for people with ova, too. The bodhisattva path is gender neutral.

It's a plus to be healthy, of course, if you want to have enthusiastic energy. I try to take good care of myself, for my own sake and for the sake of others but, vitamins and sit-ups notwithstanding, frailty is likely to come in one form or another. Even though I spend extra time working on my upper-body strength at the gym, I can no longer lift a heavy suitcase, either mine or someone else's, into the overhead bin. As I've gotten older, my arthritic joints have taught me humility: my health is not entirely under my control.

Here's the good news about virya: As my father's story demonstrates, it doesn't depend on good health. If you're alive, then joyful effort is possible. Sickness and old age don't necessarily take away your deep vigor. You can be fully alive as long as you *are* alive.

I get energy from being in the natural world, from feeling the wetness of rain, the chill of wind, the heat of sun on my skin. Weather calls me into the moment. So do plants, like the camphor-smelling eucalyptus trees rattling their leaves in Tilden Park, near my home in Berkeley, and non-human creatures like the hummingbird hovering at the jasmine, who pins me to the moment with its sharp little bill. When my energy is low, taking a walk in the woods or by the water always heartens me . . . once I get over the hump of inertia and out the door.

I was walking with a friend by San Francisco Bay this morning and suddenly we came upon a big shiny snake, a yard or so long, sunning itself on the path in front of us. It had a beautiful brown pattern on its back but no rattle on its tail, so nothing to be afraid of. It gave us time to take a good look before it slipped away into the grass. It woke us up. "Look where you're going!" it said, and so we did. Startled into the moment, we forgot what we'd been talking about before we saw it, but I didn't mind—I enjoyed the rush of virya in my veins.

When I was seventy, my long-cranky knees were giving me more trouble than ever, and I had both of them replaced at the same time. That was six months before I was planning to walk the Camino de Santiago in Spain with a friend to celebrate her sixtieth birthday. Pilgrims have traveled this route—five hundred miles across Spain, ending at the Cathedral of St. James in the city of Santiago—since the ninth century, and in recent decades the route has become popular with non-Christian pilgrims as well. It takes about a month to walk the route, but my friend had arranged for a bus to accompany us so that we could travel the whole route in two weeks, riding part of the way on the bus each day. Before signing up for the trip, I expressed concern to my friend that my knee replacements might prevent me from going, and she said I could walk the whole route on the bus if I wanted to.

Trading in two knees at once left me without a leg to stand on, and recovery from the surgery took time and effort. The exercises that follow knee replacements are painful, as their main purpose is to break down the very scar tissue that the body grows in order to protect the wounds. (Our bodies have not yet evolved to cooperate with joint replacements.) Nevertheless, I did the exercises assiduously, even with vigor. How did I, a person not brave about pain, find this zeal? For one thing, when I scheduled the surgery, I formed a clear and deliberate intention to do whatever I could for my knees. For another, the loving help I got from others gave me strength.

My sister Nora came from Santa Fe to stay with me during my first week back home after rehab. I lay on my back and raised one leg in the air. Nora is usually a kind and gentle person, but at my request she heroically forced herself to bend my knee and press my heel toward my butt, counting the seconds, pushing harder and harder until I called "STOP!" Ten times, twenty times. And then the other side. It hurt! Nora was as brave as I was to do this. We cheered each other on, and during the week she was there, we watched the angle at my knee sharpen noticeably. This was proof that enthusiastic energy can be mutually generated.

Having the Camino ahead of me was good motivation, too, and the thought of it nourished my joyful effort. I was determined to walk on that Spanish road for at least a part of every day. By the time I left for Spain six months later, I was walking about a mile at a stretch.

The first day on the Camino, our kind young woman guide kept me company at the tail of the line, and we set forth down the cobbled street out of Saint-Jean-Pied-de-Port in the Pyrenees. I grasped my hiking poles, put one foot in front of the other, and walked the two miles to our lunch spot on the bank of a stream. The others were waiting for us there, and they set up a cheer for my knees when I arrived.

Each day the path unrolled before me. We walked mostly in silence—singly, in twos, in threes—each at our own pace. I was always the last one of our group, and often someone walked slowly with me. With each succeeding day I rode the bus a little less and walked a little more, and by the last day, I walked seven miles on my new knees.

It wasn't just the mileage that brought me joy. It was the sense of being on a pilgrimage route, with other pilgrims from all over the world. The route was not crowded, and often there was no one else in sight, but we were all going the same direction, up hill and down dale, calling out "*Buen camino!*" –literally "Good road"– as we passed by other pilgrims, or, more often, as they passed us by. Most people were dedicating their journey to something meaningful for them: to someone who had died, for example, or to healing a relationship, or in gratitude for a recovery of some kind. I dedicated my journey to Margie, an old friend back home in Berkeley who was weakening from cancer, and I sent her a postcard every day. She was alive when I got home, and glad to have gotten my postcards. She died within the year.

One day on the Camino, my friend Melody was walking with me on a dirt trail through fields of fresh-cut hay that made the air smell delicious. Big bales punctuated the gold stubble, and dark gray clouds lay beyond the fields in every direction. The storm came on suddenly; the wind drove the rain horizontally into our faces and whipped our ponchos around us. My glasses were spattered with rain so I couldn't see clearly. We had to shout to hear each other above the howl of the wind.

It was hard work to keep walking, but there was nothing else to do. I was nowhere but on that path, in that place. No doubts, no wondering, *Why did I ever come on this stupid trip?* I was engaged in breathing and stepping.

At one point I had to pee. Other pilgrims were coming along behind us, so we struck out into the middle of the field and hid behind a giant hay bale, while Melody stood to my windward. I managed somehow to get the right number of layers pulled down under my loudly flapping poncho in order to pee in the storm, and then we walked on. New knees, cold rain, old friend, in Spain.

One of the heroes of my life is Fannie Lou Hamer, a Black sharecropper in Mississippi who became a leader of the civil rights movement in the early '60s. I met her when I went to Mississippi as a volunteer to help with voter registration in 1964. I was young and impressionable, and my heart was broken open by the racist persecution I saw in Mississippi, beyond anything I ever could have imagined in my sheltered and privileged life in New England. Fannie Lou Hamer had risked her life over and over as she worked for voting rights and other basic rights for Black people. She was beaten almost to death in jail in an assault deliberately arranged by the guards, and she never fully recovered her health, but this didn't stop her.

I thought Fannie Lou Hamer was the bravest person I had ever met. She didn't know me, but I knew her. At meetings, as we stood in a big circle, she often led us in singing. "We are not a-fray-ay-aid . . ." we sang along with her, even though we *were*. She was short and stout, and when she sang, her face, scarred by blackjacks, was beaded with sweat from Mississippi summer heat and her own ardor, and her voice came out of her like light. And that was her signature song: "This little light of mine, I'm gonna let it shine." Lightsaber of love. Fannie Lou Hamer gave me that song, and that energy, to carry with me the rest of my life. She was pure virya.

About twenty years later, I thought of Fannie Lou Hamer and felt virya rising in my veins the several times I was arrested for civil disobedience while protesting nuclear weapons. Another thirty years after that, I summoned joyful effort when I joined with others and spent a week canvassing to get out the vote, before each of the last two national elections. Every knock required effort, and to make it joyful, I wished each person well under my breath as I walked up to the door: "May Lupita Gutierrez be free from suffering." Sometimes I could hear a dog barking loudly on the other side of the door: "May Jake Williams be happy. And may his dog be at peace." What I was doing was not particularly dramatic. I was hot and thirsty, most people weren't home (or pretended not to be), and yet every time I encouraged someone to exercise their right to vote, my zeal grew.

I could say to myself that I'm not nearly as brave as Fannie Lou Hamer was, but that's not the point. I doubt that Fannie Lou Hamer was telling herself how brave she was–she was forgetting herself and shining. Joyful effort can't be weighed or measured. It comes forth not just when you are afraid or doing something difficult. Enthusiastic energy comes forth when you are discovering the joy of your life. It's a quality you can foster and then, if all goes well, it gathers momentum and fosters itself. It can even work retroactively: I have generated enough enthusiasm to throw myself into a cold lake on a hot summer day by throwing myself into a cold lake on a hot summer day.

Virya blows away obstructions and brushes away distractions. Virya fuels enthusiasm for the life I'm living, which includes getting older. What can I do with joyful effort in my late seventies? Lots of things, but here's an example: I can get up extra early, like I did this morning, to make bran-walnut muffins for my sister and her husband, the two other old people in the house. Last night I set the alarm to get up early enough that the muffins would be out of the oven and ready to eat before Francie and Bob came down for breakfast. Age hasn't dampened my enthusiasm for making bran muffins, nor has it stopped me from being able to do so.

But when the alarm went off: *Oh no! What's this?! Too early!* Just as I started to burrow down again, I remembered, *Oh, yes–I'm going to make bran muffins for Francie and Bob,* and I leaped out of bed. Well, my heart leaped and my body followed, in a septuagenarian version of a leap that looks a lot like standing up slowly, but enthusiastically, in the spirit of *Go for it!*

Bran muffins are nice, but what about climate change and white supremacy? What about contributing to the common good? Yes, that, too. I cultivate joyful effort to help me find my way to appropriate action in the larger world. Even though I take action in less physically vigorous ways than I did when I was young, I can still be acting with enthusiastic effort. (See the chapter "Sentient Beings Are Numberless, I Vow to Save Them" for more on activism.)

Old people tend to go slow, and that can be a good thing, because you see more of what's around you when you slow down. The pace that's right for you is the right pace. Sometimes I see a bent old hairpin of a person inching across the street on a crosswalk. I can tell that they're not going to make it to the other side before the light changes, and it's clear they can't go any faster. How brave they are, trusting their lives to unknown drivers waiting to step on the gas. That takes virya.

I heard about Captain Tom, a person who followed his own pace. He was a ninety-nine-year-old British veteran who, during the COVID-19 lockdown, walked on his walker around and around his own garden in the month before his hundredth birthday, raising money with each lap to help the National Health Service in treating COVID-19 patients. He walked slowly: one hundred laps, adding up to a total of about one and a half miles, in three weeks. That's half a mile a week, or a tenth of a mile a day with weekends off. Slow and steady. That was perseverance! He inspired people because of his age, and he raised over thirty million pounds. Happily for him, the Queen knighted him before his death from COVID-19.

You miss things when you're in a hurry. Everything happens so fast in our world that to slow down is to offer the reminder, to yourself and to those who walk with you, that each step is a precious step. It turns out that going slow gets you from one moment to the next just as effectively as going fast, as long as you don't dawdle.

Here's a verse about virya from Shantideva, an eighth-century C.E. Indian Buddhist sage who wrote the long poem *A Guide to the Bodhisattva Way of Life.*

The lichen hanging in the trees wafts to and fro,
Stirred by every breath of wind;
Likewise, all I do will be achieved,
Enlivened by the movements of a joyful heart.

Every breath. Virya comes with every breath. I'm alive until I'm not. I'll give you vim and you give me vigor. Let's walk, vote, and bake as long as we can, and shine right up to the end.

Watcher at the Gate

I WAS WITH my close friend Friedel when she died. We say the word *die*, but it doesn't tell us anything; we don't know what it is. We haven't done it yet, so how could we know? At other times, we, the breathers, say "pass on," "pass away," or simply "pass." These words imply a journey; we make a metaphor with language to give form to the formless. I don't know what Friedel's passage from life to death was like for her. What I can speak about is what it was like for me; how I, in the witnessing of it, passed from life into more life.

One afternoon, when Friedel was alone at home, her left arm went suddenly numb and heavy. It had happened a few times before, but this time it was more pronounced and lasted about twenty minutes. Fearing she'd had a stroke, she turned off the flame under the lentil soup, let in the cat, and, not wanting to trouble anyone, drove herself to Kaiser Hospital Emergency. She was German, born in 1939, and her childhood in Munich during and after the war had taught her stoicism and self-reliance.

Our mutual friend Melody phoned to tell me Friedel was in the emergency room. Melody couldn't go visit her just then, but she suggested I go check on her, even though Friedel had said she expected to be home again soon. I showed up at the hospital without calling first, so she couldn't tell me not to come. By the time I got there, the medical concern for her had grown, and Friedel was not about to go home. I sat beside her bed in a blessedly quiet corner of the emergency department, through the immeasurable afternoon and evening; in hospital time, the words *afternoon* and *evening* are no more than snatches from a forgotten song. The numbness in her arm was long gone and her vital signs were normal, but she was anxious, waiting to learn what was going on inside her. Various people came in and out, measured, probed, questioned, and left again, and in between their visits we were left alone for long stretches of not knowing.

Tests showed that Friedel's right carotid artery was seriously occluded and was probably causing mini strokes in her left arm. I was with her when the cardiologist on call said she was at risk for having a massive stroke. This was a shock. She already had a host of health problems, including Parkinson's, asthma, and heart trouble. She was seventy-five and overweight, but she exercised regularly and was tough and strong. She felt fine. And now, all of a sudden, the doctor was urging her to sign in to the hospital for surgery on the artery as soon as possible. She looked at me as if from the edge of a cliff.

Being with someone you love when they die is a classic human experience. Not so classic is being with someone you love when you suddenly realize they *might* die. Any minute. Friedel and I stood at some distance from each other now. I was too far back from the precipice to see the steepness of the drop, but she, perhaps, could see straight down. *Don't lose your balance, Friedel.*

"Think about it," said the doctor gently, "and let me know." He went to see another patient.

"What about Mitzikatzi?" she asked me. Mitzikatzi was her cat.

Had everything changed? Had nothing changed? The doctor had not said, "If you pick up the thread of your life, if you walk out of the hospital right now and go to the parking garage, drive home to your cat, turn the flame back on under the soup pot, and watch the evening news, you will have a stroke." He had not said, "You *will . . .*"; he had said, "You *might . . .*"

"I wouldn't worry about Mitzikatzi," I said. "Somebody else can feed her."

"What do you think I should do?" she said. Her question drew me into an agonizing intimacy in spite of the gap between being me and being her. I couldn't pretend we were separate.

Friedel was my close friend. We had been lovers thirty years before, and though we had discovered together that we weren't lesbians, our friendship was more deeply rooted for that long-ago exploration.

As one of my few single friends in Berkeley, she was often my Saturday-night date. We never lived together, but she was the closest to a significant other that I had in those last years of her life, and vice versa. She picked arguments with me about the movies we saw, arguments that she enjoyed and I did not. She cooked me vegetarian stew on her idiosyncratic old yellow stove. She was bossy, and she wouldn't let me light the burners; she said it was too tricky for me–you had to pull one thing and push another at the same time. Sometimes, when she was in the other room, I lit it anyway, to make us a pot of tea. I accompanied her to the neurologist after she was diagnosed with Parkinson's and took notes for her. She gave me a soft wool undershirt she brought back from Germany–special because you can't get them in the United States. She was always telling me to dress more warmly. She listened to me when I was sad or upset, and she rejoiced with me when I was happy. I learned about old-fashioned unselfishness from hanging around with her. Her loyal friendship made me feel safe in the world.

She had other close friends, too, from the various communities that she was a part of, and she was generous to everyone. Because her blood relatives were in Germany, we, her friends, were her American family.

That night in the emergency room, I saw that it was up to us—and in that moment, it was up to me—to stick by her. There was no one else in that room of white sheets and white walls—just Friedel and me. I cast out thoughts of the manuscript I'd been planning to work on that evening and surrendered myself to the call of friendship. Alongside my fear for Friedel was a release from self-clinging; my life became simple. I would do whatever I could for as long as it took.

"Why don't you spend the night in the hospital and decide about the surgery tomorrow?" I suggested. That's what she chose to do. We sat together for another long time, and finally somebody came, she told them her decision, and they made up a bed for her right there in the emergency department. I went home to sleep and came back first thing in the morning.

Friedel's chance of having a major stroke was greater if she didn't have the surgery than if she did, though strangely, the biggest danger of the surgery was that it would *cause* a stroke. I don't remember the exact numbers—something like a 4 percent chance of major stroke from the surgery and a 20 percent chance of major stroke without it.

She asked us, her friends, what we thought she should do. Some of her friends said they couldn't answer that question. How could they possibly give her advice about such a decision as this? I understood, and I almost said the same, until out of my dry mouth came the words, "I think you should go for it." I cling to the idea that I added some sort of disclaimer, like, "Do what your intuition tells you to do." I was not the only one who encouraged her to have the surgery; we wanted her to live and so we thought she should go with the best odds. Statistics seem definitive when they are about someone else's life.

Friedel wanted to live, too, but for her the numbers were numbers and her life was her life. She knew she might go home and never have a bad stroke; it was even probable. She had not been planning to come to the hospital for major surgery. She'd been in the stream of her life:

working on fundraising for her Parkinson's support group, planning dinner for a book-group meeting. She was the one who would have to give up her plans. She was the one whose tissue would be stabbed by the surgeon's tools.

I watched Friedel wrestle with this decision. Whatever her friends said, she was deciding for herself. She was a rational person, and she believed in Western medicine. This was not a struggle against doctors who wanted to sustain a severely impaired life. On the contrary, the point was to avoid severe impairment. She took the leap. She decided to have the surgery.

I was present when she talked with Dr. P., the surgeon, before he operated. A kind man, he listened attentively as Friedel went over her advance directive with him. She told him, "I don't want to survive a severe stroke. I don't want to survive if I don't have language, or if I don't have the use of my limbs, if my quality of life is severely impaired."

I was one of the people who had power of attorney for health care, whose phone numbers were given to Dr. P. Friedel had already made us promise to honor her wishes. "And if you're in doubt, let me go." That was scary for me, but at least, thanks to this instruction, I would know what to do if I didn't know what to do.

It was a long surgery.

I wasn't at the hospital for the surgery, but Melody and her husband, Mischa, sat in the lobby beside the operating room for the whole three hours while Dr. P. threaded a tube from Friedel's groin up through the artery, all the way to her neck, and put in a stent. When it was done, Melody called me to say that it had gone well, that Friedel came out of it smiling, and that Dr. P., also smiling, declared, "I'm proud of her!" Melody said, "Friedel's powerful life force triumphed!" Death receded.

When I got to her hospital room twenty minutes later to celebrate, there was a bustle of activity around her bed and nobody was smiling.

She had had a stroke immediately after returning to her room. The entire left side of her body was affected, her face was slack on that side and her speech was slurred, but she was conscious. A clot had lodged in the new stent. The Grim Reaper approached again.

The back-and-forth was terrible: getting ready to lose her, getting ready to have her back, getting ready to lose her again. I made myself imagine it. *We won't go to New York together next summer after all*, I told myself.

We have only metaphors to talk about death, but the Grim Reaper metaphor is all wrong. Forget I said it. It makes us think we're separate from death and that death is our enemy. On my bureau, another metaphor: A Mexican Day-of-the-Dead diorama, a scene in a box just a couple of inches high, in which a skeleton doctor delivers a skeleton baby from a skeleton mother while a skeleton nurse stands by. It reminds me that birth and death go together. Death keeps giving us life, killing old cells to make room for new ones. And what's hiding under my skin? My skeleton, who lies down with me at night and gets out of bed precisely when I do in the morning. Still, it was harder to remember that death was not my enemy when I feared that it would come for Friedel.

I just had time to squeeze her hand before they wheeled her back into surgery. During the emergency angioplasty, the second one in a day, Dr. P. shot massive doses of anticoagulant into the artery to "melt" the clot. It worked. Over the next few days, all the symptoms of the stroke disappeared and Friedel's speech went back to normal. Her vitality returned.

She practiced walking up and down the hospital corridor. She became exultant. She was going to be discharged in a couple of days. She called her brother in Germany to tell him the good news. Her friends visited, brought take-out food, all of us celebrating that she would be going home to Mitzikatzi. She thanked us for being a real family for her, for sticking by her no matter what and helping her pull through. And she reminded us over sushi, "Don't forget, I don't want to survive a serious stroke."

Early one morning I was preparing to visit her, putting into a bag some things she had asked for–clothes for when she was discharged, and a novel–when my cell phone rang. "Friedel" came up on the screen.

I answered. "Hi, Friedel, I'm just getting ready to come and see you."

"I'm sorry. This is not Friedel. This is Dr. P."

My heart lurched. He told me, gently, that Friedel had just had a massive stroke. There had been extensive bleeding in the brain and she was now completely unresponsive. He said, "Do I have your permission not to intubate her?"

I managed to ask in words I don't remember whether she could possibly recover, and he said no. If she lived, she'd be completely helpless.

Even though there was no question in my mind about what to say, even though any one of her dear ones would have said the same, still, in that life-and-death moment of accountability, my mind searched wildly for an overlooked escape route for Friedel, as if there might be a passageway through heating ducts in the hospital basement. How could I break the spell that had been cast upon her and get her, alive and laughing, out of the hospital and back to her lentil soup?

I was alone in my bedroom, holding on to the telephone, with no one else to refer to. Here was another chance to express my love. A choice that was not a choice. Friedel and I were not separate in that moment, though she was dying and I wasn't. I had no doubt about what to say, and I was grateful for that, but I had to take responsibility for saying it. I had to be brave for all of us. Allowing Friedel to die forced me to grow up, to go beyond myself.

"We have to let her go," I said through my parched throat.

Dr. P. said she'd probably "pass" in a few hours.

Friedel, still alive, was lying on her back, mouth open, eyes closed, freed from the tangle of tubes and technology that could no longer help her, and the skin of her face looked soft and smooth. Her breathing was labored. A paisley shawl I had given her was spread over her torso. I and four other close friends stood around her bed and sang old songs and took turns holding her hand. One friend came with copies of the *Heart Sutra*, a Buddhist chant, and a few of us chanted it together. Friedel was not a Buddhist, but I don't think she minded. *Gate, gate, paragate, parasamgate, bodhi svaha.* (Gone, gone, gone beyond, gone to the other shore. Oh, awakening.) The chant encircled us as we encircled Friedel. It comforted me to chant something that humans have been chanting for about two thousand years, a chant about the impermanence of our separate lives and how there are no boundaries between us.

Friedel was breathing raggedly and the nurse gave her some morphine, but it didn't settle her. A little more and her breathing quieted. We kept telling her we loved her, in case she could hear us. She was alive, with us, even though she was unresponsive.

Then she stopped breathing. The nurse felt for a pulse and shook her head: "She's gone." We stood still and silent as our tears came. One of her friends said, "This is the saddest I've ever been in my whole life." We sank back into silence, and half a minute later, Friedel exhaled with a loud burp. We all jumped with fright. The nurse said that often happens–it was just the release of the air left in her lungs. Her mouth gaped open and a trail of mucous came out of one corner.

What the nurse said–and the *Heart Sutra*, too–was true. She was "gone." Her body was in the same spot, but everything was different. A body of absence lay on the bed. Where did she go–the one who had been breathing? And not just where, but how? How did she get out of here?

It seemed we stood there forever. Death is outside of time. It takes the person who dies out of time, and it took us, the living, out of time, too, for a while that was neither long nor short. We kept standing there, and we cried, and we looked at each other, and each one of us kissed her forehead that had turned pale in a moment. You could say there were five of us around her, but we were not a number, not countable. We were not distinct from each other.

During that last week of Friedel's life, the wheels of love had been gathering momentum as we kept coming to cheer her on. By the end, as we stood around her bed, the air in the room was the substance of love. The blankets and chairs and even the various pieces of medical machinery that she was now blessedly unhooked from—everything was made out of love. I saw that that's what matters: to give oneself away to love. In the midst of uncertainty, love is certain.

The death of someone close to you is like an alarm bell: *Wake up! This is it! Do what you care about! Love is what matters!*

If you've been present at both a birth and a death, you know it's the same gate, whether it says "Entrance" or "Exit" across the top. How do you know? If you get up close to the person who is being born or dying, you can get a fleeting glimpse through the gate to the horizonless expanse on the other side, and it looks the same whether they are coming or going.

When my own children were born, my body became the gate and my legs were the two pillars of that gate. The first time, I had the only obstetrician in Boston who practiced "natural childbirth." On the delivery table, with all my attention focused on riding the towering wave that was my son's life coming, I heard the doctor say, "Push, Susan! Push for the Czechoslovakian interns!" Only then did I notice the ring of visitors around the table who had come to observe what we then called a "natural childbirth" and was still unusual in a hospital setting at the time. I pushed, but not for them—they were welcome to be there, but they were not what interested me just then. I pushed for the life that was straining to come out of me. I pushed until my child's face swam into focus, the face I hadn't been able to see before he was born.

Death is nearby, at birth. Three years later, when the second child came through the gate, this time in Berkeley, his newborn face was blue and he was silent. "Why isn't he breathing?!?" I shouted. The doctor siphoned out his nose and mouth and gave him some oxygen, and after a few seconds, which lasted a few years, the baby began to holler, his face turned a beautiful red, and his small heart pumped new life into the whole universe, so that when we left the hospital to go home the next day, all the plum trees in Berkeley were in bloom.

I stroked Friedel's forehead, warm under my feeling hand and then quickly cold. Her skin was pink to my seeing eyes and then it was white. Feeling and seeing were gone for her.

I knew somehow: Friedel's okay, now that she's dead. She doesn't have to be afraid anymore of being partially paralyzed by a stroke. I knew, too: I'm alive, and it's my job to be alive while I am alive, whether I'm okay or not. That's my assignment from Friedel.

My aliveness grew so large in that moment that the boundaries of my body could no longer hold it in, and it poured through unknown seams and cracks into the room. No longer mine, no longer my separate life.

Getting Over Myself
in the Monastery

WHEN AT THE AGE of seventy-six I told my friends and family I was going to spend a three-month winter "practice period" as a monk at a Zen monastery in the wilderness, they were not sure this was a good idea. I wasn't sure it was a good idea, either.

For ninety whole days, I and my fellow Zen aspirants would tuck ourselves into a narrow valley—no coming, no going, relinquishing ordinary comforts and pastimes, rising long before the sun, and following a demanding schedule of meditation, study, and work.

A few decades before, I'd been to a winter practice period at Tassajara Zen Mountain Center and I'd experienced moments of vastness. I had also known the three great challenges: cold, sleep deprivation, and unremitting zazen (the Zen form of seated meditation). When I had returned to civilization, I continued to practice Zen with stubborn devotion, but as time went on, thoughts of another practice period fell away: too old (me), too cold, too hard, too far from loved ones.

But when I learned that my longtime teacher Norman Fischer and his wife, Kathie Fischer—both of them old friends, and I mean both kinds of "old friends"—would be leading a practice period, I set my heart on going. Other dear friends from my Everyday Zen group in the Bay

Area were going to be there, too, and I trusted Norman and Kathie not to drive us past endurance. Here was a chance, almost certainly a last chance, for me to experience a long retreat among supportive dharma brothers and sisters. Maybe this time I could give up self-clinging once and for all. In the Ventana Wilderness, a place empty of email, cars, and deadlines and brimming with the stillness of people sitting together, I might even come to understand the point of my life, just in the nick of time, before I got to the end of it.

Getting ready involved buying rubber boots, formal Zen robes, and other items from a long list sent out from the Zen center. It's remarkable how much equipment is required to live as a Zen renunciant in the wilderness. My preparations also included getting my everyday world ready for me not to be in it. My email vacation message read: "On retreat, no email. Please contact me again after April 4." I passed on bill-paying and business matters to my sister Francie and brother-in-law Bob, who live with me. I kept saying to them, "I feel like I'm getting ready to die."

"I wish you'd stop saying that!" Francie said.

But in preparing for the practice period, I *was* practicing dying. I was giving my loved ones, and maybe even myself, a preview of me being gone.

So it was that I packed my duffel bags full of long underwear and robes and squeezed into a van, along with a half dozen other eager and apprehensive monks-to-be, to make the epic journey to Tassajara. The last couple of hours were on a long dirt road through the mountains, in pouring rain. As we came over the high saddle, we saw before us not the clear day's view of receding ridges getting bluer and bluer in the distance but a heavy curtain of rain, hiding everything from view except a steep bank on one side of the road and a sudden drop-off on the other. This opacity was the gate we had to pass through. Our skillful driver, a resident monk, drove us into the storm and down the steep and winding slope, with windshield wipers squeaking, and delivered us safely to Tassajara on a cold and muddy January day. I wouldn't see the other side of the mountain for ninety days.

I was in a different world. No daily news, no talk of Trump. We were all suspended in ancient Japanese Zen time, marked out by bells and drums and a wooden mallet striking a wooden board.

The wake-up bell roused us at 3:50 a.m. to days of meditation, study, and work at our assigned jobs, with a break before supper for bathing or exercise.

As Buddha mentioned, if you don't make a fuss about getting what you want all the time, you'll be much happier, but if you cling to the desire to stay in your cozy sleeping bag as the wake-up bell is clanging in your ears, you're heading down a rough road.

I came to Tassajara wholeheartedly, wanting to release my grip on preferences. I wanted to stop worrying about whether what I was doing was the very thing that I most wanted to be doing. Clearly, the older I got, the more frequently I would experience unpleasantness. I saw that it behooves an old woman to learn to roll with the punches. So, every morning when the wake-up bell rang, I rolled.

I got into my robes as quickly as possible and staggered through cold and dark to the "samovar" in the outdoor courtyard, to have my life-supporting cup of green tea before zazen. Dizzy from lack of sleep, I took my personal mug from the pegboard and fumbled with ungloved hands to open the jar containing the tea bags and get one into my cup. Biting down on my flashlight, I held my mug in one hand and opened the spout of the samovar with the other. On rainy days, the routine was further complicated by my umbrella. So much for elegant Zen simplicity.

I took my tea into the dark dining room and sat in silence among the shadowy shapes of a few other regulars at this pre-zazen café. Over the months, I learned to recognize which of my fellow monks they were by the way they hulked in the dark over their coffee or by the sound they made clearing their throat. An unspoken alliance grew among us but was never spoken of. This was one of my favorite parts of the day.

After my tea, I walked down the path, beyond the zendo (the building used for meditation), toward the baths, to breathe the morning air. I moved my body in its heavy robes quickly through the dark cold canyon, like a swimmer, and paused to look up at the stars in the narrow angle of sky, as bright here as anywhere I've ever been. And when the moon was full or newly waning, its early morning brightness filled the canyon and lapped on the zendo roof like water. I had only a minute or two to walk before the sound of the han, mallet on wood, called me back to the zendo. No one else seemed to do this. It was my secret treasure, this walk in the dark. It helped me stay awake for the first few minutes of zazen.

Every fifth day we had what was called a "personal day." It used to be called a "day off," but they changed it because there's no such thing as a day off from life. On personal days, early-morning and late-evening zazen framed a day of free choice—what a challenge! Nobody told you what to do. You could nap, visit with friends, hike, write letters, read, do your laundry, nap again.

To keep a connection with my three young granddaughters—two six-year-olds and a twelve-year-old (no FaceTime at Tassajara!)—I vowed on every personal day to write a postcard to each one of them—Sally in Ohio, and Lali and Caleb in Texas—telling them something about my life as a monk. I looked forward to this writing project every personal day.

Dear Sally—I was sweeping the dining room floor this morning, and another monk told me there were some ants in the corner, and he asked me not to sweep there so that I wouldn't kill them.

Dear Lali—Every time you meet someone on the path, you bow to them. What if you bowed to whoever you met on the sidewalk in Austin? That would be strange, wouldn't it?

Dear Caleb—You don't really need a watch here. When it's time to get up, someone runs past your door clanging the wake-up bell. When it's time for zazen, someone hits a wooden board with a mallet. When it's time for work meeting, someone rings a railroad bell. Time passes calmly. You don't have to rush, but you can't be a dawdler, like someone I know in Texas.

The greatest physical challenge, much harder for me than the cold, was the lack of sleep. If all went smoothly, you could get about six hours of sleep on regular nights. In monastic settings, both Buddhist and Christian, there seems to be a traditional belief that lack of sleep is good for your spiritual practice because it humbles you and weakens your ego. Yes, it humbled me, but it did not help my spiritual practice. My constant torpor was a kind of hell. My heavy head fell forward repeatedly, I was tormented by swarms of one-second dreams, and I jerked awake again and again with a cramped neck. During the two periods of zazen before breakfast, I fought sleep and lost, over and over. I was often sleepy during the day, at lecture and study hall as well as zazen, and the last two periods of the day, after supper, were a dead loss as far as spiritual practice was concerned. My body cried out: *Please let me lie down! Please, oh please.* I felt like I'd been surreptitiously drugged, or like somebody had hit me over the head with a sledgehammer, or like I was drowning. Sometimes I really thought I must have narcolepsy. It wasn't my fault!

And yet to my own surprise and even satisfaction, I found the stamina to follow the schedule. "Following the schedule" is a sacred tenet of the practice period. I kept dragging my body back to the zendo, sleepy or not, while chanting inwardly, *No picking and choosing! No picking and choosing!* I'm not sure how useful this was, but at least I proved that I wasn't a quitter. I was the second oldest monk in the valley, by just a few months, and even if my chin was on my chest, I was no slouch. But who did I think I had to prove it to? Well, in addition to me, myself, and I, there was the *tenken*–that's the person who takes attendance at every zazen period and comes to find you in your room if you're absent, supposedly to find out if you're sick and need anything. Part angel of mercy, part truant officer.

I was one of a half dozen chair people. We, the most arthritic, sat facing the wall in the corners of the zendo, as if we were being punished for not sitting cross-legged on a cushion, though really the corners were the only place to put the chairs. I had sat for years in half lotus until my knees gave out and I got a new pair. The new knees were great for walking, but cross-legged sitting still wasn't possible. Sometimes, in my chair, my back or my neck did not feel wonderful, but intense physical pain from long hours of sitting was no longer a problem, as it was for most cross-legged sitters. I was grateful for this.

Mental pain, however, was my companion. When I wasn't asleep in the zendo, I worried. I had several soundtracks to listen to. *Isn't it selfish of me to spend three months contemplating my navel in the mountains?* In Berkeley, friends were demonstrating on behalf of people seeking sanctuary at the border. *Shouldn't I be there with them?* I focused on the coolness of the air as it entered my nostrils and the warmth of the air as it left–a remarkable change. But what good did that do asylum seekers?

I worried further: *I'm too old to benefit. This is supposed to be a training monastery, but I've been practicing Zen for over forty years. What do I think I'm "training" for at this point? It's one thing to come here as a young person, to learn how to open up your eating bowls and where to put your chopsticks, to deepen your practice for the years ahead. But what am I supposed to be learning so close to the end of my life?*

Worse yet: *If I haven't gotten it yet, I never will. I'm not capable of awakening. I can't go deep. My meditation is a joke . . .*

The afternoon work period brought respite. I had the job I had requested: kitchen crew. Every afternoon, about six of us donned aprons, bowed to the kitchen altar, bowed to one another, and for the next three hours we did as the *fukuten* (kitchen manager) told us. For example: "I need four people on bok choy. Ten gallons, medium rough chop." Only "functional speech" was allowed in the kitchen.

The fukuten was a young woman, very curt with me for the first few days. "No, that doesn't go there!" And she'd hurry off without telling me where it *did* go. At Tassajara, where not a lot of exciting events happened from one day to the next, every personal interaction was magnified a hundredfold. What I heard her say was, *You are a shuffling and slow-witted old woman!* The third or fourth time she scolded me, this time for using the wrong-colored sponge to wipe the cutting board, I summoned my courage: "I just got here. I need some time to learn."

"Me, too," she said. "I just started this job." Then I put myself in her shoes and saw that she was nervous herself. She was working hard at a stressful job, like being the stage manager of a theatrical performance, coordinating many interdependent tasks, in which timing is everything, culminating in the exclamation, "Serve-up in five minutes!"

"I don't know how you do it," I said. "I'd be a total wreck if I had your job."

"I'm sorry I was abrupt with you," she said. "I don't disrespect you."

Dear Sally–They keep the kitchen knives really sharp here. There's no talking in the kitchen, but when you're walking through the kitchen carrying a knife, you're supposed to call out, "Knife!" to warn people, so nobody bumps into you.

I soon got to know my way around the kitchen and felt at home there. We all worked together: four of us cutting beets, for example, two on each side of the counter with our cutting boards and knives, and in the middle, a big white plastic five-gallon bucket that needed to be filled with the beet slices and a metal bowl for stems on their way to the compost. We were one animal with eight arms, cutting, reaching, sliding slices into the bucket, without words—a soft percussion band making pleasant knocking sounds of knives chopping on wood, occasionally punctuated by the equally pleasant *ching* of a scraper striking the rim of a metal bowl.

I had to pay attention, but I didn't have to think. I didn't have to decide anything. The beets chased away my worries as the bright slices fell away from my knife. I could see the white bucket filling with red, and I knew I was helping to feed the sangha (our community of monks). Once, for fun, I carved a slice into the shape of a heart, and that night at supper, miraculously, the server spooned that very heart out of the pot and into my little bowl.

We learned kindness from each other. Every other day, the afternoon kitchen crew was responsible for mopping the kitchen floor. This unpleasant job included carrying the heavy rubber floor mats outside to the porch and hosing them down, and sloshing the heavy rag mops around a floor that was sprinkled with onion skins and blobs of dough. Almost every mopping day, the same two guys on the kitchen crew volunteered for the job. I knew they didn't particularly like doing it, because in the first days, they waited a couple of beats before offering themselves up to the task. Later, they just did it. I admired their practice of no preferences. It could have been thanks to the example of these dharma brothers that I volunteered one day for the big spring-cleaning job of washing the kitchen windows, which involved climbing up onto the high tile counters, reaching into grease-encrusted corners, and wiping away dead insects from the sills. It was awkward work, but it brought a little more light into the kitchen, and that was pleasing. In addition to the ego satisfaction of feeling noble, I can honestly say that I was glad to be saving someone else the trouble. We trained each other in generosity.

For a week each month, we had a *sesshin*, that is, a meditation intensive during which we followed an even stricter schedule than usual: zazen all day, clothed all day in robes and silence. Not even the relief of afternoon work periods in the kitchen. In our first sesshin, in the days full of sitting, I involuntarily fell into a sort of life-review process. This can be a positive developmental stage for old folks, but I was often looking through my habitual lens, reciting my old regrets to myself. I thought of my failures in love, my mistakes as a mother, my unfinished writing projects. I thought of how lonely I had been and sometimes still was, and how I had practiced Zen for decades and still didn't "understand the Great Matter," as one of the old Zen masters put it. Many tears landed on my chest. *Dammit,* I said to myself, *I* knew *this would happen!* There was no slicing of beets to pull me out of my misery, as could happen during my afternoons in the kitchen.

You will think me mad that I wanted to do this practice. But I have to tell you that all the while, I was glad to be there. Some faith in the dharma sustained me, in the form of blue jays calling into the silence, or a line from the morning service–"The stone woman gets up to dance"–or the evening offering of a hot ginger drink in the warm and silent kitchen. I could think myself unhappy and yet rejoice at the sound of the rain on the zendo roof. The jays, the incense smells, the round of days and bells.

I had my first meeting with Norman during that sesshin. I told him about my tormenting sleepiness, which was not even alleviated by naps. I told him about my familiar demons, my sharp regrets, my chasm of longing. I told him I'd tried to do too many things in life and so I had never become my true self. These are the kinds of thoughts that a person like me can build up into a giant edifice when she is in silence all the time and nobody's stopping her. I told him, "I don't know why I'm here. I'm too old; it's too late." Norman, who had heard my stories plenty of times before, said it was wonderful that I was there–I'd come to the perfect place at the perfect time to finally face the loneliness and regret and go beyond it. He even suggested that the sleepiness was a defense against this encounter.

I came away from that meeting with renewed intention. Yes, I was lucky to be there. Yes, it wasn't too late to be my true self. Let the demons come if they would. I would not hide.

So I sat. Painful memories came up from nowhere, helter-skelter, but I didn't let them unseat me. It was as if something shook the library shelves of my brain and forgotten books fell open on the floor. In zazen and even during meals, the past was often my present. I was in the yellow house on Parker Street, crouching in the coat closet so my husband and small children couldn't hear me crying. I could even smell the coats when suddenly, as if through a peephole in the closet door, I saw a lunch server standing in front of me in the zendo, waiting for me to hold up my bowl for a scoop of rice.

Meeting what came took guts—I give myself credit for that. Curiosity helped me, too. I was amazed by the vividness of the past, by the tenderness of my children's skin when they were babies, by the collapse of time into one moment, by the smell of the diaper pail in my monk nostrils.

Outdoor walking meditation helped me. Every day in sesshin we followed our head student in a long line: a black centipede winding up the road, beside the rushing stream, our black back warmed by the sun thanks to a welcome break in the weather. I watched the long body climbing the road ahead of me, the body that I was part of. Then the centipede doubled back in a U-turn, and the body slid past itself until it unfurled into one long line again, and we aimed our many legs back down the road toward the temple roof below us. The air was fresh. I wasn't separate. I didn't have to speak.

Once in a while, in zazen, I was present in the room. It would just happen. The stories I told myself lost their juice, turned to dust, and blew away. My arms hung comfortably from the coat hanger of my shoulders. I could feel the actual warmth of my living brain inside my skull. I listened to the stream that couldn't stop singing, and to the jays, who stopped and started. I was sustained by the invisible pulse of my shadowy fellow monks, breathing all around me, all of us like swimmers in the half light, sharing the time that was given to us by the sound of the stream. Each time I sank back down into the sucking bog, I believed in it a little less. Its grip was weakening.

One of the challenges of the practice period was being stripped of one's identity. We were all indistinguishable, in our shapeless, genderless black robes, stepping over mud puddles on the way to the zendo. I learned to recognize people by their hats, the only idiosyncratic item of clothing allowed—red wool or tam-o'-shanter. Whatever roles I played in the world beyond—writer, teacher, mother, grandmother, sister—were gone. And that's the idea—you take a shortcut to finding your true nature. But sometimes I felt more like I was rediscovering my adolescent nature, as though I was starting in a new high school where no one knew me and I had to figure out how to present myself as a likable person. There were times when we monks could talk to each other—on personal days, on workdays, and at our weekly informal meals in the dining room. At first, we were like strangers meeting on the train. And when a few people thanked me for my writing, I was startled by the reminder that I was much too old to be in high school. I was an elder with a long life behind me. I confess I was relieved to have part of my identity returned to me, even if it overlaid my deeper buddha nature.

For three months, sixty-four of us lived together in that cold and stormy valley. We ate together, studied together, listened to dharma talks together, bowed and chanted together, worked together, sat in silence together. We were "alone together," as the Zen expression goes. At the beginning of the practice period, the weight of that expression was on the word *alone*. By the end, it was definitely on the word *together*.

At our formal meals in the zendo, we each opened our own set of three cloth-wrapped bowls and laid them out before us according to an intricate choreography dating back a thousand years or so. I loved this part. Most people ate their meals in cross-legged zazen posture, putting their bowls on the meal board directly in front of their seats. But we chair-sitters ate at individual tables, like little TV tables, which a server brought to us at the beginning of each meal.

The servers for the day carried heavy pots of steaming food out of the kitchen building and up the stone steps into the zendo, in dark or daylight, in rain or wind or mist or freezing cold. (I had opted out of being on a serving crew because I was afraid of tripping and dropping a pot of soup during this difficult journey.) We chanted the names of Buddha while the servers ladled food into our bowls

I found the food delicious, except for the time I accepted a large helping of undercooked turnips, thinking they looked tasty, and I was compelled to hide them in the capacious sleeve of my robe to dispose of later. But here's the amazing thing: I had three meals a day for ninety days—that's 270 meals in a row, cooked and served for me by the sangha. How could I not be overcome by gratitude?

At Tassajara, I noticed things that were usually hidden from me by the stimulation of life in the outside world. For example, while I was wrapping up my bowls at the end of a meal and the servers were running alongside the meal boards, wiping them off with a damp cloth, I could actually feel my digestive juices squirting into my stomach, and I realized that I was, in the broadest sense, still eating. Or when I concentrated on the rushing of the stream, the sound pulsed slightly. How could I not have noticed this before? Outside the zendo, I tried to find some sort of obstruction in the stream that would cause a series of sound waves, but I could find nothing. I finally realized that the pulsing was exactly in sync with my heartbeat and the sound was caused by the rhythmic circulation of blood in my ears. I was hearing my life in my ears.

Dear Lali–Before I go into the baths, I chant our Buddhist bath prayer: "With all beings / I wash body and mind / free from dust, / pure and shining, / within and without." Do you think you can wash your mind in the bathtub?

The sangha, our village of monks, helped me. We helped each other. I certainly wasn't the only one who struggled with demons of one sort or another. I doubt that anyone there was demon-free for ninety days in a row.

Sometimes, on a personal day, I would invite someone to go for a walk with me–a friend, or someone I wanted to know better, or someone who seemed in need of companionship. It was a pleasure to give encouragement as well as take it. I caught on to the fact that, thanks to our shared commitment to practice, every person there was Buddha, just different years and models. We had a big age spread, from twenty-three to seventy-six (me and another woman). The connection between old and young was fruitful. The old were inspired by the ardor of the young and their eagerness to devote themselves to the good. The young were inspired by the steady perseverance of the old over the long haul, demonstrating that Zen is something you can do for a long time.

Each of the students who was there for the first time gave a "way-seeking mind talk," telling the story of how they came to be a monk at Tassajara. When the young ones gave their talks, I was struck by the number of them who had recently been in desperate straits. Only a year or so before, some had been oxycodone addicts, or serious alcoholics, or ski bums with no sense of direction but down. Some had been suicidal. One young man told of deciding, while in community college, to become a junkie on purpose; he said he didn't know who he was or what he was doing, and being a junkie would at least give him an identity and even a kind of purpose. He told us, between sobs, that he nearly died from an overdose but that his younger brother, who adored him, saved his life.

Instead of preparing secure financial futures for themselves, a logical pursuit in one's twenties, these young people had come to the boondocks of Tassajara for the sake of something more important to them–to find meaning, community, their own aliveness. I could see them changing before my eyes, and they reminded me that I can change, too. An old dog *can* learn new tricks, it just takes her a little longer than a young dog.

I never thought for a moment of leaving Tassajara. Impossible as it seems, I was happy, in a deep, abiding way, even when I was most dejected.

As I listened to the stream, the sound of time passing, I began to let go of regrets. A voice in my head, probably mine, declared, *There's no such thing as "If only I had . . ." If-onlies don't exist! What had happened had happened; if-only had not happened. I'm old but I'm not dead, and it isn't over yet.*

I saw that I'm actually not nobody. I've put a self together over my long life, with the help of my genes and good fortune and everyone I've ever met, and I walk around in this self, impermanent and at the same time real–friendly, conflict averse, curious, self-deprecating, sincere, wanting to love, wanting to be loved. I saw that it's a good-enough self for everyday life. *So give yourself a break, Sue–it's okay!* What's more, this self, while real, is not the whole deal; my buddha nature is there underneath regardless–a big self beyond liking and not liking.

One day it came to me that the last part of my life was the perfect time for me to be at Tassajara. This practice period could help me accept the life that's gone before and help me be truly alive until I die.

One day, toward the end of the practice period, two fellow monks–both dear dharma sisters–and I were cutting heads of cauliflower into florets to fill a five-gallon bucket. There was no one else in the kitchen and so, like three unsupervised children, we fell into conversation. I said, "I'm feeling guilty for not volunteering to wash dishes when the fukuten asked."

My friend Jaune said, out of the blue, "Oh, just get over yourself, Sue!" It was so unexpected, so unlike her kind self, that I was undone. It came like an arrow straight to its target. But had I really heard her right?

I looked up from the cauliflower to see mischief at the corners of her mouth, and before I could think, I burst out laughing. "That's it!" I said. "That's exactly right! That's the whole point of being here!" All at once I was flying. *Get over yourself, Sue.* In my white apron, with a green bandanna tied around my forehead to keep my hair out of the food, I was soaring over the kitchen roof, getting over myself, above and beyond the old-fashioned turbine ventilator that rotated in the wind.

At the same time, down in the kitchen, we were still putting florets into the bucket. My friend Ruth said offhandedly, like an ancient Zen master tossing me an instruction, "It's a koan." We all cracked up then.

In the days that remained, I often told myself, "Just get over yourself, Sue!" And every time I said it, I felt happy.

> *Dear Caleb—The practice period will be over in a few days, and this is my last letter to you from Tassajara. Buddhism has taught me what you already know, that love is the most important thing.*

It could have been the next day. In the early morning dark, walking in my robes to the zendo for meditation, I looked up at the bright stars and saw Orion, his dog at his heels, leaning over me as if protecting me. I called up: *Thank you, stars, for letting me be in the universe! Thank you, big bang, for getting the whole thing going!* I gave them a big shout-out. The stars reached across the millions of light years between us, from another eon all the way to my retinas.

At the very end of the practice period, a departing monks ceremony was held for those of us who were leaving the monastery and going back out into what's known as the world–back to the brouhaha, back to our cell phones and loved ones, back to the onslaught of disturbing news.

It's a privilege to be part of a Zen practice period; most people don't get to do what I had done. True, most people wouldn't want to, but some who would dearly like to be monks can't spare the time or the money. Yes, money: you have to pay to be cold and tired.

For three months I had lived in close community. We'd shared our sincere intention to practice and our packages of chocolate from home. We'd studied the teachings together and sat in silence together. I had felt safe. I had been sheltered from multiple forms of pollution; relieved of responsibility; given a chance to pay attention to my body, my breath, my thoughts and feelings, and to notice their impermanence.

I had wanted to give up self-clinging. Had it worked? Was I different now than when I entered? Would I be more able to help others?

In the ceremony, we departing ones circled the inside of the zendo in a procession, our palms together, our torsos bent forward in a humble half bow as we passed by the seated forms of our teachers and the monks who were staying on. It's hard on the back to walk like this, but it felt right to show my gratitude in this way. Someone read our names aloud, concluding, "You return to the marketplace with gift-bestowing hands." It was a statement, not a question. May it be so.

Make Your Body a Sundial

All things in the entire world are linked with one another as moments.
—DOGEN, "THE TIME-BEING"

BUDDHA SAYS step up to the plate right now, in this very flash of the pan. This is it, kiddo. And yet, in a seeming contradiction, we Zen people frequently chant the names of our ancestors, turning our attention to people who are nowhere in sight at the moment, who lived hundreds and hundreds of years ago. Decades ago, when I took vows to keep the Buddhist precepts, I was given my lineage paper, kind of like an American Kennel Club pedigree—ninety-two generations of ancestors who passed the dharma along, from Buddha down to me.

When I first started practicing long ago, the emphasis on lineage rubbed me the wrong way. On my car I sported a bumper sticker that read Question Authority. In those days I thought that meant "Don't bow to dead Zen teachers." I supposed that they were from too far back in the past to have much relevance for my life in the more important present.

But I kept going back to the zendo, and one of the "ancestors" I met there was Eihei Dogen. Chanting his thirteenth-century words while the incense stick burned down on our twentieth-century altar, I saw that Dogen was trying to help me, and he didn't care whether I bowed to him or not.

Zen Master Eihei Dogen was born in Kyoto in 1200, the illegitimate child of a woman of the Japanese imperial court. Dogen's mother died when he was eight, and it is said that as the orphaned child watched the incense smoke ascending at her funeral service, he experienced the impermanence of all things. He could have grown up to hold a high position at court, but at thirteen, longing to seek the truth, he became a Buddhist monk. Dogen was the founder of the Soto school of Zen in Japan, and he is known for his extensive philosophical and poetic writings.

I live a long way from that orphan boy in thirteenth-century imperial Japan. I grew up as a daughter of privilege in New England, seven and a half centuries later, eight and a half thousand miles away. What a miracle that Dogen's writings are so central to me and my explorations of what it means to be a human being. The dharma flies past the calendar at the speed of light. Dogen's teachings from long ago are alive in us in the present.

Every year I celebrate Thanksgiving with the same group of extended family and friends. None of these people are Buddhists, but at some point during the long meal, I make everyone stop talking; I stand up from the table that is laden with turkey and sweet potatoes, and I read to them from Dogen's "Instructions for the Tenzo." (The *tenzo* was the head cook in a monastery.) When I first get up to read, my friends and relatives groan affectionately, muttering, "Here comes the lecture about the rice and the eyeball." But they have come to appreciate Dogen, too. His words are an expected part of our ritual.

I tell them how Dogen says we should take care of our rice as though it is our own eyeball, and we should prepare food with kind mind. "Kind mind is parental mind. . . . You should look after water and grain with compassionate care, as though tending your own children."

And then, to make them laugh, and because I want them to know that the Buddhists of the past were human beings like us, I read from

Dogen's "Instructions for Taking Food": "Do not look into other monks' bowls, arousing envy. . . . Do not throw balls of rice into your mouth."

My niece Sasha, now grown, tells me that sometimes, in a restaurant, she finds herself looking over at another customer's plate and wishing she'd ordered that. Then she says to herself, *Do not look into other monks' bowls, arousing envy.* So it turns out I'm passing Dogen's teachings along! I'm in the lineage, and Sasha's in the lineage, too. If the ancestors of the past want to talk to the generations of the present and the future, it's our job to help them do it. We can carry their teachings from another time and place right to the family table.

———

Each moment is all being, is the entire world. Reflect now whether
any being or any world is left out of the present moment.
—DOGEN, "THE TIME-BEING"

It's all here, right now, in me and around me, in what Dogen calls "the time-being." I think of the time-being as vertical time, in contrast to chronological, sequential time. The ancestors are here with me right now and the babies who haven't been born yet are here now, too, already walking and talking.

In the fall of 2011, I spent a day with the Sacred Sites Peace Walk, led by Japanese Buddhists and Native Americans. The walk's twofold purpose was to honor and protect Native American sacred sites and to raise awareness about the dangers of nuclear power. These two purposes were braided together as one: honoring the ancestors of the past and taking care of the ancestors to come.

We visited a Native American burial ground near Mission San Jose, where Indian people were buried in unmarked graves. We stood in a circle on the bumpy grass, and a wand of burning sage was passed around the circle for healing. The Ohlone leader Corinna Gould told us that they had recently reburied a baby there–a baby two thousand years old–because its remains had been dug up, along with the remains of other ancestors, to make room for a housing development. I wondered, *How could a baby be two thousand years old?* We each made an offering of a pinch of tobacco at the center of the circle, as three young Indians drummed and sang. I thought about the little body going into the ground and out again and in again, the little bones coming apart over the years. Our ancestors were babies. Our babies will be ancestors. It's our job to take care of them.

———

Do not think that time merely flies away. If time merely flies
away, you would be separated from time. . . .
—DOGEN, "THE TIME-BEING"

At this moment in time, I see my granddaughter as an eight-year-old child, and she sees me as an old woman, an ancestor. She also makes real for me the need to take care of the future–that's where she will be living, along with all the other children who make it there. I know her now, and if I'm lucky I'll know her as a young adult, but I won't know her when she's a middle-aged person. That's a strange feeling. She won't be very old at all when I die. So she travels far beyond the threshold of my life. She may even have a granddaughter some day, and she won't know her granddaughter as an old woman either.

My grandmother had a shelf of children's books that had been hers when she was a child, back in ancient times, as I thought. I loved to turn the fragile pages and look at the children playing with their hoops and tops. The books were so old and yet, strangely, they were for children, who had been as young as me when they read them. I was also fascinated by my grandmother's old photo albums, in which I saw my father as a child–on horseback, in a sailor suit. There was magic in looking at him as a boy.

Every once in a while, my granddaughter says to me with amazement, "You're my dad's mom!" She's trying to absorb this remarkable truth. It's a mystery to me, too.

In our arrogance we sometimes think that history begins with us, forgetting how our lives depend on the struggles of those who came before us. But our predecessors have looked out for us in ways both known and unknown. Not all of them, of course, but thanks are due to the ones who did. What about Lucretia Mott, who fought for the vote for women? What about Frederick Douglass, who helped bring about the end of legalized slavery? Or Rachel Carson, whose work led directly to the banning of DDT? We might want to chant their names as ancestors. Or the people who wrote the Bill of Rights? What about the people who established Social Security? Or Sojourner Truth, who struggled for abolition and women's rights? If we want to be helpful to the ones who will come after us, let's show a little gratitude to the ones who came before. How hard is that? We're links in a beautiful chain. Hey, we're part of a parade!

———

The mountains, rivers, and earth are born at the same
moment with each person. All Buddhas of the three
worlds are practicing together with each person.
—DOGEN, "ONLY BUDDHA AND BUDDHA"

In Werner Herzog's film *Cave of Forgotten Dreams*, I saw the oldest cave paintings yet discovered, dating back thirty-five thousand years ago. And yet the horses are still whinnying across the walls of the cave, nostrils flared, eyes wide, alive. And the Andromeda Galaxy you see tonight in the telescope was doing its dance three hundred thousand years ago—long, long before the charcoal horses ran. If beings riding on another planet around another star are watching us, they may not see the smoke from the Fukushima Daiichi nuclear power plant disaster for tens of thousands of years.

Astrologers study the configuration of the heavenly bodies at the time of a person's birth. It seems possible that the way everything is lined up at the moment when a person is born would affect the unfolding of that person's life. When the stars assume a certain pattern, that's when a person is born; and when a person is born, the whole universe comes into being. Each birth completes the pattern of the universe at that moment.

Here's another mystery. At the time that I was born, the sun was in the constellation Scorpio. That's how the stars lined up in the sky on that date. The brightest star in Scorpio is Antares, six hundred light-years away. So doesn't that actually mean that the sun had been in Scorpio six hundred years *before* my birth? The now of my birthday and the now of Scorpio don't match. Or to look at it another way, this is further proof that it's all one big Now. My birth took place in all time. Yours did, too.

Stand under the sun and make your body a sundial. Watch your shadow swing around you. Turn yourself into an hourglass. Let the sand run down your spine. Chronograph, timepiece, keeper of the calendar–you are nothing but time.

There is not, after all, a contradiction between being here now and remembering the many generations behind us and the many generations to come. I like the feeling that my life is a leaf in the generations of leaves. My life is a leaf. I'm a link. I'm a blink.

When I get away from my appointment book, from busyness, when I sit down for a drink of water beside a stream in the sun, I feel completely present. I watch a lizard skitter under a rock. At the same time, I feel how huge the mountains are and how long their lives, how tiny and brief I am. A bright flash in a pan.

Knowing How to Be Satisfied

I vow not to take what is not given, but to be satisfied with what I have.
—NOT STEALING, SECOND OF THE TEN GRAVE BUDDHIST PRECEPTS

Money can't buy back your youth when you're old,
Or a friend when you're lonely or a love that's grown cold.
The wealthiest person is a pauper at times
Compared to the man with a satisfied mind.
—PORTER WAGONER, "A SATISFIED MIND"

THE FIRST OF Buddhism's ten grave precepts is against killing. The second is against stealing, and at the heart of not stealing is a sense of gratitude. Everything in our world, everything in our lives, is already given to us. I'm breathing the air that surrounds me, my heart is beating without me having to remind it.

Almost fifty years ago, someone made an offhand comment to me: "Oh, if you're interested in Zen, there's a Zen center in Berkeley." When I walked up the stairs of a Victorian house on a busy street, and up some more stairs into the attic, there under the rafters was the zendo with its bells and cushions; there was Buddhist practice waiting for me. What a generous universe.

I'm grateful to Sojun Mel Weitsman for starting the Berkeley Zen Center in the '60s and to the many others who have worked hard to keep it going. All I have to do is get myself there. We have to cooperate with the universe in accepting what it offers us.

What is given to us is the chance to become human beings together. Even the challenges and the difficulties are given to us. We didn't ask for these challenges, but they are given, and what is given is a gift.

The Korean Zen teacher Seung Sahn encouraged his students to have what he called "enough mind." To have the attitude *I already have everything I need*. He said that when you want something you don't have, there are two possible outcomes, and both result in suffering. If you don't get what you want, you suffer from disappointment. If you *do* get what you want, you can experience temporary happiness, but pretty soon the happiness fades when it turns out that what you got isn't quite as wonderful as you expected it to be. You begin to crave all over again, and you are right back in the cycle of craving and suffering.

I want to whisper something in your ear, though, that Seung Sahn didn't mention. Once in a while, you get something you want and it turns out to be as wonderful as you expected, or even better, and it makes you happy for a long time, maybe all the way until you die. Don't worry too much if that happens to you; it won't stop you from having "enough mind."

Buddha and his followers were great list-makers. I suppose it's one of the things that attracts me, an enthusiastic list-maker myself, to Buddhist teachings. One of Buddha's lists is "the Eight Awarenesses of the Enlightened Person," and one of the items on this list is "knowing how to be satisfied." I assume it's on the list because Buddha or one of his friends noticed the human tendency to remain stuck in a sense of insufficiency.

I used to feel lonely, and I suffered because I felt lonely. In between relationships that turned out to be temporary, I was pained by my lack of a life partner, and I blamed myself. I couldn't keep myself from envying the imagined happiness of friends with partners and then, adding insult to injury, I would give myself a hard time for doing so. But I began to understand that measuring my happiness against the happiness of others is senseless. They might be envying me for something, too. I can't tell by looking at someone what they have and what they lack. They might have demons inside or a history of loss that I can't imagine.

Now, happily, thanks to aging, to dharma, to my Zen sangha and my community of friends and family, and to a change in living arrangements, I don't bother myself about being single anymore, not hardly ever. I gradually caught on that underneath the loneliness was a deeper problem. That problem, as I have been reminded by a Zen elder or two, was my belief that I should feel some other way, in this moment, than the way I feel. It's a given that I *will* feel some other way, maybe quite soon, but in the meantime, it's like this now. Whatever unhappiness comes, can I say to myself, with this inhalation, *I have what I need in this particular second*? Can I say it again as I exhale? And then, by all means, I'll do my best to remedy the situation, if remedy there be.

Many people really don't have everything they need. They lack food, shelter, warm clothes, health care, education, and a safe environment in which to raise their children. It would be extreme arrogance to suggest that a refugee mother interned in a camp with her cold and hungry children should tell herself that she has everything she needs. How we work against the institutions that put her in that situation, how we build social structures that bring everyone the essentials they need to sustain life, these questions are "beyond the scope of this essay," to use a phrase that sounds uncomfortably like an excuse. But what I am talking about here—a bottomless feeling of lack—is connected. And I'm talking about greed, also connected. We live in a society that encourages us to want stuff we don't really need. The advertising industry colludes with our sense of insufficiency to turn us into unintentional thieves.

In Buddha's time, it was easier to know if you were stealing. You knew where the thatch of your roof came from. You knew who made your clothing. Your food was mostly locally grown, and you took your water from the stream or the village well. Now the sources of our food and drink and the necessary materials of our lives are from invisible sources. We might be stealing without knowing it. The teak trees that were cut down to make the furniture on my back porch–were they truly offered, or were they taken from protected forests? The labor of the women who made the jeans I'm wearing–was that labor truly offered, or was it from sweatshops where women worked in exploitive conditions close to slavery? At this point in human history, we can't always avoid taking what is not given, but we can try to live as simply as possible.

Voluntary poverty is an aspect of various kinds of religious practice. It's so much easier to focus on what's important when you aren't worrying all the time about maximizing your choices. I know from people more advanced than I am that there's freedom in simple living. Besides, the more of us who use less, the better for all life on planet Earth.

I can't pretend I'm practicing voluntary poverty, but I do find that the older I get, the simpler my needs are and the more easily I feel satisfied. This is particularly clear in the material realm. I don't want *more* stuff; I want less. Old age is also a time for downsizing ambitions and dreams along with material things. Not only do I accept the idea that I will not travel to the amazing ruins of Machu Picchu before I die–something I actually used to want to do–but I'm now quite *satisfied* that I will not be spending vast sums of money on being cold and uncomfortable and suffering from altitude sickness. I don't look for ecstasy anymore; a walk by the bay with a friend is wonderful enough. Yesterday we watched a great blue heron promenade with long-legged dignity along the water's edge. It was quite exciting.

I-have-everything-I-need is a restful feeling. I'm not acting out of a sense of lack.

I still have to watch myself. I have to watch out for garden-variety stealing, for taking what's not given in small ways. A case in point: I was traveling with a dharma sister a few years ago, leading some Zen retreats in Europe, and we were staying in a hotel in Prague that offered a huge complimentary buffet breakfast. Our last day there, we had breakfast in the hotel before a long day on the train to Berlin. I finished my eggs and croissants, and I said to Cynthia, "I think I'll wrap up some croissants and cheese in a napkin for lunch on the train." She looked at me with surprise, noticeably taken aback. She challenged me, gently, saying, "Do you think that's being offered?"

"It would hardly make a difference," I said. "It would be as if I had had a really big breakfast." But she said, "What if everybody said that to themselves? What if everybody in the hotel used this buffet as the breakfast *and* lunch buffet?"

I imagined myself watching another hotel guest–a gray-haired, pleasant, well-behaved woman like me, for example–going back to the buffet table, wrapping up some croissants in a napkin, and tucking them into her purse. I wouldn't report her to hotel security, but watching her do what I was about to do, I would be able to see that she was taking what was not given. It would be like seeing myself in a mirror. Cynthia had held up that mirror.

"You're right," I said to Cynthia. "You're absolutely right. Thanks for helping me with the precepts." It was a small thing, but it made an impression on me. The point was not the couple of croissants I didn't take but rather that with Cynthia's help I cracked a habit–the habit of thinking that I'm a good citizen, so it must be okay. I was reminded that I'm not different from other people. There are no separate rules for me.

This is like the classic minor theft of taking home some pens and paper from the office supply closet at work, with the justification that what people don't know won't hurt them. If nobody experiences being hurt by it, if nobody even *notices* it, why not? As with the croissants, the problem here is the attitude more than the pens–the idea that it doesn't count if no one sees you do it. But it counts if you see yourself do it. This sounds sanctimonious, but it really does count. The precepts are not commandments handed down to us from the outside but affirmations that come from within. They are the intentions of our hearts.

Even though I have everything I need, I still have longing. I'm not so satisfied that I can take a permanent rest from learning and growing and changing. My turn for that will come in due course. For now, while I'm still alive, I'm still reaching out for connection.

There's a difference between craving and longing. It's a wholesome longing that brings me to spiritual practice, a positive hunger that calls forth *bodhicitta*–the arising of the thought of enlightenment for oneself and others. There is a Zen saying: hunger is a monk's staff.

Years ago, when I was lamenting to my friend and Zen teacher Norman Fischer about my bottomless longing that was never satisfied, he said that longing is its own satisfaction. That was a big help. Longing is what I do. It's who I am. My longing leads me through one gate after another, in the general direction of connection.

In his influential essay called "*Genjokoan*" ("Actualizing the Fundamental Point" in English, or, roughly, "manifesting the heart of the matter"), Dogen speaks about how the self and the whole universe are one, and how everyday life and deep spiritual practice are not separate. What are probably his most familiar lines come from this essay: "To study the buddha way is to study the self. To study the self is to forget the self. To forget the self is to be enlightened by all things." Thanks, Dogen, for reminding me that I am made out of everything in the universe, that I am interdependent with everything, that my very atoms are made out of stardust.

Another aspect of longing, besides the longing for connection, is the longing I experience to be my full self, to offer whatever it is that I have to offer during my short individual life and to do so without holding back. It's a longing to be creative, something that I believe is part of our nature. We are makers. We give back, and in doing so we move beyond our small selves. The question becomes not "Am I getting enough?" but "Am I giving enough?" Am I giving myself away fully to this life, this precious human birth?

Ryokan was a Zen monk, hermit, and poet in eighteenth-century Japan. One evening he returned to his hut on the mountain after visiting a friend and he came upon a thief looking for something to steal. But there was nothing to take. Ryokan said, "You have come a long way to visit me, and you should not go away empty-handed. Please take my clothes as a gift."

The thief was bewildered. He took the clothes and slunk away. Ryokan sat naked, watching the moon. "Poor fellow," he said to himself. "I wish I could have given him this beautiful moon." Then he wrote this haiku:

> The thief
> Left it behind—
> The moon at the window

So there's no such thing as stealing in the face of complete generosity. And what is truly valuable, the light of the moon, a symbol of enlightenment, cannot be stolen.

The practice of generosity is a great help in cultivating a feeling of sufficiency rather than lack. Every fall, our Everyday Zen sangha has a two-month period of intensified dedication to practice. One year I decided to take up the practice of generosity in a deliberate and practical way for these two months. Every day I gave away something tangible, something that belonged to me or something that I made: a good book, a pair of earrings, a pot of soup. It was challenging to find the things to give away and the people to give them to. I couldn't just knock on my neighbor's door and say, "Here's a brand-new toothbrush still in its wrapper that I got from the dentist as an extra and I thought you might like to have it." No, I had to consider what a gift is. It was a good exercise because it made me flex my gift-giving muscle, even if it was in a contrived way, and it underscored the truth that the greatest gifts I can give are not objects. The greatest gifts are time, attention, and, well, what we call love. But giving away tangible things encouraged me to be generous in those other ways as well.

I recommend this exercise to you, too. It's not the way to equalize the distribution of wealth in our society, but it's a way to explore your own feelings about giving. Commit yourself to a specific time period and be respectful of the recipients of your gifts. Don't ask anyone to accept, out of politeness, a gift they don't even want.

I practiced a variation of the same idea many years ago, for forty-nine days after my father's death. Forty-nine days is the traditional mourning period in Buddhism, and in the Tibetan belief system, it's the time it takes for the departed to find their next rebirth. My vow was to give money, even if only a quarter, to every person I met who asked for it, on the sidewalk and the street. In a mysterious way, it helped me honor my father and grieve his passing. In Buddhist terms, you could say I was dedicating the merit of my small offerings to my father's safe passage. I tried to always have quarters and dollar bills in my pocket and in my car, so as to be ready to give to someone in front of the grocery store, or to reach my arm out the car window to someone on the median strip when I stopped for a red light. You could take up this practice for any length of time and for whatever reason. If you do, say to yourself each time in the moment of giving, as I tried to do, *This could be me.*

Shantideva was an eighth-century Buddhist monk in India. In his great text *The Way of the Bodhisattva*, he writes about generosity and

what he calls the exchange of self and other. This is one of my favorite
verses:

> If I give this, what will be left for me?
> It's thinking of myself, the way of evil ghosts.
> If I keep this, what will be left to give?
> Concern for others is the way of heaven.

One more story about stealing. A few years ago, I was on my way
to Arizona to co-lead a women's retreat. I took the BART train from
Berkeley to the San Francisco airport, the last stop. I had my carry-on
bag beside me on the floor. But when I got to the airport, I reached for
my carry-on bag and it wasn't there. It contained my laptop, phone,
IDs, credit cards, cash, address book, appointment calendar, and all my
teaching notes. Stunned, I reported the theft to the BART police at the
station and made my way to the United Airlines counter, grateful that
at least my plane ticket was electronic and had not been stolen. I could
borrow a toothbrush in Arizona. But the agent wouldn't let me board
because I didn't have any ID to go through security. As far as United
Airlines was concerned, I wasn't anybody at all. At least I had my subway pass in my pocket, so I didn't have to beg for my train fare. I took
the long BART ride home again, and as it turned out, I was able to fly to
Arizona the next day, using my passport as ID.

But here's the point of the story: Riding the train home from the airport, in a state of shock, I felt stripped of everything. I looked out the
window at the hills of San Bruno rolling by and I suddenly thought, *Hey!
The thief didn't steal my life. The thief didn't steal my body. I still have
my family and friends.* I touched my own knees in amazement. I wanted
to jump up and down in the train, shouting, "I'm alive! I'm alive!"

The theft was a strange kind of gift. I lost some objects, yes, some
important objects, and I gained a sense of gratitude for my life that is

still with me. I often forget how amazing it is to be alive, but if I concentrate, I can open a drawer in my mind and find the memory of that BART train ride: *I'm alive! I'm alive!*

In the deepest sense, nobody owns anything. We will all have to let go of everything when we die. In the meantime, whatever we have is already given to us. I'm going to hold my so-called possessions loosely, without clutching. I have everything I need at this moment.

We Will Be Ancestors, Too

ZEN PEOPLE TALK a lot about how great the Buddhist ancestors are. As I have said before, I used to take a dim view of the whole business of honoring ancestors. I loved my grandparents, but not because they were "ancestors." When I first began to practice in my thirties, I was impatient with the emphasis on the "lineage," a long list of dead men's names from India, China, and Japan. About fifteen years ago, thanks to pressure from women practitioners and our male allies, we began chanting the names of women ancestors as well as men in our formal Zen services, a historic turn. But in my early days, I thought the lineage a dusty business, like a pile of tattered diplomas on crumbling parchment, having nothing to do with me or my life.

Now I realize that the ancestors are my lifeblood. We are all made of the ancestors who came before us, those who bore us and those who bore the ones who bore us, all the way back through the generations to Great-Grandmother and Great-Grandfather Amoeba. Some of our ancestors may not have been admirable people, but we come from them, too, whether we like them or not. People who are adopted may not know who their blood ancestors are, but we come not only from blood ancestors but also from the people who raised us, who taught us to look both ways before we crossed the street and how to tie our shoes.

I'm here because of all the teachers—the first-grade teacher who taught me to read, the sixth-grade science teacher who taught me the ten-point scale of hardness from talc to diamond, the high school and college teachers who helped me love Shakespeare and George Eliot. Come to think of it, Eliot and Shakespeare are themselves my ancestors, as is everyone who handed on the culture that shapes my consciousness without me even knowing it. I'm talking to you now, thanks to the *Homo sapiens* who first used words, and their descendants who kept passing the language along until it got to me—language that organizes what I see and hear: dark, light, square, round, soft, and loud.

I acknowledge the many people who have been robbed of knowing who their biological ancestors are because the link has been broken by slavery, genocide, war, displacement. There are also people who have been robbed of their cultural and spiritual ancestors, as the past has been torn away from them. There are people who honor and receive guidance from the tree ancestors, the ocean ancestors, the mountain ancestors, and the star ancestors.

When Florence Caplow and I were compiling a book about wise Buddhist women of the past, I came to admire all the women ancestors we included in the book, especially Satsujo, a serious Zen practitioner in eighteenth-century Japan. I was initially drawn to her because she was a grandmother, and I'm a grandmother, too. As I studied Satsujo and came to feel connected to her, I made a great discovery about ancestors: you can adopt whoever you want as an ancestor. You don't get to choose your biological parents and grandparents, but when you're adopting ancestors, you get to invite people you admire—the teachers, historical figures, writers, and artists who have influenced you and encouraged you—to be your ancestors. They're not going to turn you down. I have adopted Satsujo as a third grandmother, and I take her with me as I go through life. I identify with her more as I get older, and she's my friend as well as my ancestor. Wanting to get to know her better, as one does with a new friend, I learned what little I could about her life.

Satsujo's father studied Zen with the great Rinzai teacher Hakuin, and even when Satsujo was a small child, she used to go with her father to see Hakuin. In this way, she became a sincere student of the dharma at a young age, and she continued to practice and study with Hakuin all her life. She was a laywoman, wife, mother, and grandmother, and she taught Zen informally. Hakuin was known for being kind and encouraging to the people in his village, including the women, despite the intensely patriarchal culture of Japanese Zen at that time. He took Satsujo seriously even though she was a woman, and a laywoman at that.

Several stories about straight-talking Satsujo have come down to us. This one, from *The Hidden Lamp*, is my favorite:

> When Satsujo was old, she lost her granddaughter, which grieved her very much. An old man from the neighborhood came and admonished her: "Why are you wailing so much? If people hear this, they'll all say, 'The old lady once studied with Hakuin and was enlightened, so now why is she mourning her granddaughter so much?' You ought to lighten up a bit."
>
> Satsujo glared at her neighbor and scolded him: "You bald-headed fool, what do you know? My tears and weeping are better for my granddaughter than incense, flowers, and lamps!"
>
> The old man left without a word.

As a mother and grandmother, I can't think of a sorrow greater than a beloved child's death. It seems to be against the natural order of events. A grandmother should die many decades before her granddaughter, as any grandmother worth her salt would agree. But I believe a person who doesn't have any children or grandchildren of their own can imagine this sorrow, too. This story is for everyone.

Apparently the old man thought that if Satsujo was enlightened, she wouldn't cry over her granddaughter's death. That's like saying that if you're enlightened, you won't be a human being anymore. Satsujo didn't turn away from her human feelings. Tears are precious. Tears join us to those we love, whether they are living or dead.

When one person tells another not to cry, it's almost always because they are made uncomfortable by the tears. From the weeper's point of view, being told "Don't cry" is *not* helpful. An old pop song pops into my head (you have to be old to remember it): Lesley Gore, in 1963, when she was seventeen, singing It's My Party "and I'll cry if I want to." Both Satsujo and Lesley were defiant about their right to cry. Satsujo's grief was of a different order than Lesley's, but, yes, it's Lesley's party, and it's Satsujo's party, too. They were each in wholehearted attendance at the party of their human life.

The more I consider this story, the crosser I get with the old man, because his chief concern was *what people would say* about Satsujo. He was more worried about her reputation than her sorrow.

Satsujo shows me that an awakened old Zen adept and a broken-hearted grandmother can be one person. She says, *Trust your tears. Go ahead and light some incense and offer some flowers if you want to. But it's the salty river of your grief that flows straight to your grand-daughter, wherever she is.*

How do you weep without getting lost in weeping? I'm guessing that sometimes you can't, but in this case, Satsujo clearly manages it. "You bald-headed fool!" she says, pausing the flow of tears for a moment. She is being completely herself, straightforward in the midst of her sorrow. She's telling it like it is, poking a hole in the old man's self-righteousness. She calls him a bald-headed fool not because there's anything wrong with being bald–people with a head of thick hair can be fools, too–but because she's upset with him for caring more about reputation than love. She is, admittedly, rude.

Satsujo knows that grandmothers need to grieve for their grandchildren. What sort of a world would it be if they didn't? When our hearts are broken, we need to cry. Getting intimate with Satsujo, I stand a chance of catching her courage, her wit, her trust in herself. She teaches me not to cramp my true self with ideas of who I *should* be and how I *should* act. She encourages me to cry, out of love. And to call out the fools and tell it like it is.

Zen Master Dogen, in thirteenth-century Japan, had a young student named Tetsu, who was a very serious practitioner with excellent zazen practice and perfect comportment. He recited the sutras fluently and did everything he was asked to do. But he was short on compassion. Before Dogen died, he told Tetsu, "You can understand all of Buddhism, but you cannot go beyond your abilities and your intelligence unless you have *robai-shin*, grandmother mind, the mind of great compassion." Dogen's phrase *robai-shin* has been translated variously as "grandmother mind," "parental mind," "kind mind," and "compassionate mind." In his "Instructions for the Zen Cook," Dogen says that monks should have the spirit of parents or grandparents who, "without regard for whether they themselves are cold or hot, shade or cover the child." As for Tetsu, he later became abbot at Eiheiji, Dogen's temple, and I like to think this was possible because he cultivated grandmother mind.

If a young male monk can develop grandmother mind, then a person of any age, gender, and social status can develop it. You don't have to be a grandmother to give your coat to someone shivering in the cold. A particular nod of recognition is due to all the grandfathers who are devoted to their grandchildren. Grandmother mind is simply a figure of speech. Even grandfathers can have grandmother mind.

During the early weeks of the coronavirus pandemic, I spent a lot of virtual time with my grandchildren: Lali, 7, and Caleb, 13, in Texas; and Sally, 7, in Virginia. They were not in school, and their parents, both academics, were teaching from home. I missed the kids, and I wanted to be helpful, so until their schools got some online teaching programs up and running, I talked with the kids almost every day on FaceTime. As time went on, and online classes began, we reduced the frequency of the calls to twice a week. At this writing, a year later, the kids are still in remote learning only and our calls continue.

How do you extend grandmother mind to children via pixel? How do you curl up on the couch with a first grader and read aloud remotely? How do you hug them without hugging them? I worked hard to come up with games and activities we could do on FaceTime, without being in the same room together, and for the Texas kids the games had to be what both a seven-year-old and a teenager would enjoy. Choose a few pieces of fruit from the kitchen and draw faces on them to make a family portrait. Go into the backyard and photograph all the different kinds of bugs you can find and text me the pictures. I mailed them crisp dollar bills from the bank, and after the letters arrived I showed them how to make origami hearts out of dollars. Sometimes they entertained me. When I ran out of new ideas, we turned to our fallback activity of twenty questions. The last time we played, Caleb confounded Lali and me. In response to the traditional first question, "Is it animal, vegetable, or mineral?" he replied, "All three." Down the line I asked, "Can you see it?"

"Every time you open your eyes you see it," he said. *Hmmm* . . .

Lali asked, "Is it in the universe?" But no, it wasn't in the universe. *How could this be?!?* More questions. Finally, we closed in on it. It was Lali's turn again: "Is it the universe?" Yes, it was the universe.

"But's that's not fair!" I objected. "You said it wasn't in the universe."

"It isn't *in* the universe," said Caleb in a reasonable voice. "It *is* the universe." A short ontological debate followed, and Caleb persuaded Lali and me that you never say a thing is inside of itself. "Is this glass in a glass?" he said, holding up a water glass in front of the iPhone camera. Okay, he had a point.

The seven-year-olds, Sally and Lali, in their respective homes, liked showing me things they could do. I cheered for Lali, a budding gymnast, when she demonstrated her back walkovers and roundoffs. Sally read stories to me that she had written and illustrated, about children with magic powers. The calls were surprisingly intimate. After a few months I noticed that I was getting to know the kids in a new way, watching the changes as they happened. One day loose teeth were wiggled for me, another day I saw the space they left behind, and a few calls later I saw the new teeth coming in. I saw a purple cast appear on a broken arm, and some weeks later I saw the arm again without it, and then I got see the bruise from the cast disappear. I saw hair go suddenly from long to short and then not so suddenly get longer, get cut again, get dyed blue. I saw the blue fade. Their faces were right in the palm of my hand, even though they were so far away. Our calls stretched my grandmother's heart all the way to Austin, Texas, and further east, over the Blue Ridge Mountains to the little town of Lexington, Virginia. Even when there are obstacles to expressing your love, like being miles apart in your bodies and having only a flat screen as your meeting place, grandmother mind doesn't give up easily. Grandmother mind finds a route.

So, too, if you are visiting a friend in prison and you are seated on opposite sides of bulletproof glass and you have to shout to be heard, *robai-shin* will keep reaching out until it passes through the glass. Or if you are visiting your mother in intensive care, and she has a ventilator and can't carry on a conversation, just trust yourself to your own loving intentions and you will find alternate expressions, like giving her a foot rub or singing her that song she liked about the Erie Canal. Grandmother mind is the mind of great compassion and it's for all of us.

The other side of honoring our ancestors is remembering that we ourselves will become ancestors, whether we like it or not. One of my favorite Zen texts is "Old Dogen's Prayer," or "*Eihei Koso Hotsuganmon*," in which he thanks our ancestors for their great compassion and care for us, and he assures us that we, too, will be buddhas and ancestors.

> Buddhas and ancestors of old were as we; we in the future
>> shall be buddhas and ancestors. . . .
> Those who in past lives were not enlightened will now be
>> enlightened.
> In this life, save the body which is the fruit of many lives.
> Before buddhas were enlightened, they were the same as we.
> Enlightened people of today are exactly as those of old.

We are, inevitably, the ancestors of all who come after us, whether we have progeny or not. Isn't this reassuring? The respected sages of former times were human beings with human feelings and foibles, too. They were stubborn, or bossy, or afraid. They burned the rice and spilled candlewax on the sutra book. They snuck out of the monastery in the middle of the night to do mischief. Whatever. I've been and done some of those things, and Dogen says I'll be an enlightened ancestor even so. In the meantime, in this life, I need to take good care of my human body because, whether or not it's the fruit of former lives lived by me, it's definitely the fruit of former lives lived by others. My life is the fruit of all my ancestors' lives, and my life is the fruit of the lives of the cows who gave the milk that made the yogurt I had for breakfast this morning, the fruit of the lives of the unhatched chickens in the eggs, of the carrots and beans, and even the fruit of the fruit, the organic strawberries I put in the yogurt.

So as not to waste all the lives that have donated themselves to my life, I take care of this body, and while I'm here I try to be fully here. I try to develop the mind of great compassion. I practice grandmother mind. Playing with my grandchildren, I try not to make the mistakes I made with my children. With grandchildren, it's easier to think, *It's all good!*

I try to become a good ancestor. I say to myself, *Satsujo was like me. I, in the future, will be Satsujo.*

Here's another grandmother story, about Sally. Sally had her sixth birthday while I was on my three-month intensive retreat at Tassajara Zen Mountain Center, mentioned earlier in the book. I couldn't go shopping for a present or order her something online while I was there, so if I wanted to send her a birthday present, I had to make it. She knew I was spending the winter in the cold and rainy mountains and getting up extremely early in order to put on robes and meditate most of the day. We couldn't talk on the phone; I couldn't explain to her why I would do such a strange thing. I wanted to connect with her, so, in addition to the postcards I sent her, I made her a cloth doll, over a period of a few weeks, using my precious breaks and a couple of days off. The doll, about twelve inches high, was a portrait of Grandma Sue as a monk.

Sewing has always been an important, even sacred, activity at Tassajara, because it's traditional for Soto Zen people to sew their own robes and other ceremonial garments. Monk rag dolls are not traditional, but I felt my doll was infused with Zen power. I had to scavenge all the materials. For the doll's body, I sacrificed an extra wrapping cloth that went with my set of ritual eating bowls. The stuffing for her body was extracted from a burst pillow that was on offer in the "goodwill closet," her blue button eyes were the inessential collar buttons poached from an old plaid shirt from the same place, her black robe was made from an old T-shirt, the braided cord belt for her robe was cut from the end of my own robe belt, and her aura of furry white hair, which was very like mine, was made from a frizzed-up silk scarf that I found in the lost and found. With a red felt-tipped pen, I drew a heart over her heart. As I made the doll, I was making myself. I took shape as a Zen monk in my own hands. And when I put the package in the monastery outbox, I was excited to be sending a present of my Zen self to Sally. I didn't feel so far away from her.

My son told me later that when Sally showed the doll to a friend of hers who came over to play, the friend said, "I'm scared of that doll. She looks like a witch."

Sally said, "That's not a witch, that's Grandma Sue, and she's a monk at Tassajara." I can imagine her tone of voice–definitive, announcing something perfectly natural and something to be proud of. Maybe when I'm really her ancestor gone beyond, she'll come upon the doll and think of her ancestor, the sometimes Zen monk. If their new dog, Milo, hasn't chewed it up in the meantime.

> Buddhas and ancestors of old were as we; we in the future shall
> be buddhas and ancestors.

When I say "I in the future will be Satsujo," I'm saying that I, like the rest of my cohort, will be an ancestor to all who come after me, not just to my own blood descendants or people who knew me. And they will be ancestors to those who follow them. I'm not saying that there will be stories recorded about this distinct me in future dharma books or even that my grandchildren will tell stories about me to their grandchildren after I'm gone–though, if I happen somehow to get word of it, I'll be touched if they do. I'm saying that time will take me beyond my personal self to join the river of buddhas, the continuity of the dharma.

Since we will become ancestors after we die, whether we like it or not, we might as well practice now by loving the beings we meet with grandmother mind, even if we aren't grandmothers and even if they aren't children.

Thanks for being my ancestor, Satsujo.

Friendship Abides

MY FRIEND JENNY points at a live oak tree at the edge of the parking lot. We've just arrived at the church where our weekly Buddhist seminar meets. It's twilight, when light and shadow get mixed up together. "Look," she says, in alarm, "there's a person up in the tree!"

I can't see anybody, but when we walk closer to the tree, I see a shadow where she's pointing. "I think it's just the way the streetlight is casting shadows into the tree, where some big branches cross." She agrees.

———

For years, Jenny was the one who drove me, in her old Plymouth, to our dharma seminar. An excellent driver, she was a Detroit girl who knew her cars. She used to say things like, "Look at that old Falcon! I haven't seen one of those for a long time." When Jenny's car died of old age, she decided not to get another, for ecological reasons, and so I started driving us in my car. She helps navigate, reminding me when to change lanes in preparation for an exit. This is helpful, and I need her even more for another reason. I've stopped driving alone at night for fear of falling asleep, my drowsiness having increased with my age, and she keeps me awake by talking with me. I feel safe with her.

This is how we have gotten to know each other, Jenny and I: riding in the car, first hers and then mine, to and from our Zen studies, forty minutes each way, week after week, year after year.

———

Jenny tells me more about people appearing in trees. She often sees them in a big tree behind her house. She takes me around the block so I can get a better view. But I still can't see them, and she can. This is disappointing to her. It's a conundrum. They look real to her.

———

Jenny lives alone and likes it, in a cozy little apartment full of books and her beautiful collection of pottery. She's independent and brave. She retired about a decade ago, and shortly afterward she went to Spain and walked the Camino de Santiago pilgrimage route by herself. She was in her sixties. She carried everything she needed on her back and stayed in the simple hostels for pilgrims. She fell in with walking companions along the way, while their rhythms matched, but she herself was her main companion. I wouldn't be brave enough to do that alone, even if I could speak fluent Spanish, as Jenny does. I'd be afraid of loneliness. But for Jenny it was a spiritual pilgrimage that took her beyond fear and loneliness. She gave herself to the road. She walked the whole "French Way," about five hundred miles. Two years later, she walked the route from Seville to Santiago, a little longer.

Jenny is not given to lavish expression. Her style is understated, and she never makes a fuss about herself or her accomplishments, but I know these journeys meant a lot to her; both times she came home strong, elated, and amazed, looking forward to going again. She was preparing to go a third time, on the Portuguese route, when her knee started bothering her and she canceled her plane tickets. After that, Jenny's Camino window closed, and she accepted it, with sadness but without bitterness.

———

Her eyes are getting bad. She has trouble reading, which is one of her greatest pleasures. She got a new prescription for glasses, but they don't help much.

———

Jenny and I meet in her apartment to discuss a Buddhist book we've chosen, as we have done almost every month for several years. After small talk over a delicious dinner of polenta ravioli made by Jenny and a green salad made by me, we turn to this month's book, *The World Could Be Otherwise* by Norman Fischer. Jenny reads a passage she likes, slowly, because it's hard for her to make out the words: "The practice of patience amounts to something quite simple: just keep going." She changes chairs to get closer to the light and continues, this time more smoothly: "Don't let anything that happens, including setbacks of any sort, deter you. There will always be setbacks. So whatever is going on, whatever catastrophic thing occurs, just remember: Be of benefit to others." She says she likes this passage because it reminds her of the Camino. "You just keep going," she says.

———

Jenny tells me she was looking out the window at dusk and she saw a young man hanging around in front of her neighbor's house across the street. The neighbor is away, hiking the Appalachian Trail, and Jenny feels protective of the house. She has a key and does her laundry there. She says, "I walked across the street to see what the guy was up to, but when I got close to him, he turned out to be a rosebush!" She's laughing.

———

Jenny thinks the trouble is with her eyes, because the people that only she sees are always in shadowy places where the light is shifting. I drive her to her ophthalmologist, a kind and skillful man, part of our Zen community, who examines her eyes and says her vision is compromised by cataracts and by a macular problem that is essentially inoperable, and he says, yes, this could cause her to see things that other people don't see. He says it's natural, when vision is impaired and the brain can't recognize shapes, to make sense of them by filling in the blanks and turning them into something known. At his recommendation, Jenny makes an appointment for cataract surgery.

Visitors begin to show up in the hallway of her building and inside her own apartment. They often come from faraway, or long ago, usually at night. Even when they come by day, her friend who lives across the hall can't see them. Some are more welcome than others, and some are complete strangers who sleep on her sofa. "They just grab a pillow and put their head down," Jenny explains.

Jenny has had a couple of falls, as well as increasing word loss. At the encouragement of her friends, she makes an appointment with a neurologist. I drive her there, to keep her company and take notes. Dr. T., whose mane of long red hair challenges my concept of a neurologist, is kind and friendly as they discuss what Jenny is experiencing. She congratulates Jenny on her physical health and her presence of mind, but she's concerned about Jenny's struggle to find the words she needs and her perception of people unseen by others. The doctor mentions the word *dementia* as if in passing and asks Jenny to come back in a few months. In the car on the way home Jenny is subdued.

"How do you feel?" I ask.

"I don't really want to talk about it," she says.

"At least it's a good thing that you have a connection with a neurologist now," I say. I always want to turn somebody else's bad experience into a good experience. I'm trying to learn to let it be hard if it's hard.

———

Jenny has the cataract surgery, and it helps a little, but her visitors keep visiting. When we speak of them, that's what I call them, "visitors," not "hallucinations," because I want to respect that they are real in her life. She herself knows, some days, that they are not real in my life or the lives of her friends. Sometimes she calls them "magic people." Sometimes she says they come out of her mind.

———

One warm autumn day I sit with Jenny on the front porch of the big old house in which she has her tiny apartment. She spreads an old-fashioned flowered tablecloth over the wide porch railing and sets down cups and spoons. I watch a squirrel leap from branch to branch in the oak tree next to the porch while Jenny fixes a pot of Richmond Park Blend, a British afternoon tea we are both fond of, and a plate of shortbread cookies she bought at the nearby bakery for this occasion.

"Thank you for this beautiful afternoon tea on this beautiful afternoon," I say. We're facing west, but our eyes are shaded from the rays of the low sun by the house across the street. Next to the house, a blazing-red liquid amber tree is backlit by the sun.

"My mother came today," she tells me. "I was just waking up."

I know her mother died a few years ago. "Has she been visiting you a lot?" I ask.

"No," says Jenny, "she's dead."

"Yeah, my mother visited me a couple of times after she died," I say. "Do you remember while you're talking to your mother that she's dead?"

"We don't talk about that. She comes, but she doesn't say much. I talk to her softly, but sometimes she doesn't answer." After a quiet moment, Jenny continues: "There are a lot of people around today. Sometimes as many as four people sitting on the sofa. They're not real, but they're coming up. It's a strange thing."

She tells me that when she mentions these visitors to her living siblings, who phone her often, they don't believe her. She says, "I can hear it in my sister's voice and my brother's voice. I am just beginning to hear that. You know, I don't want them to be afraid of me, or even pity me, or any of that."

———

I go with Jenny to her second visit to the neurologist, along with her friend Barbara, a retired social worker who has experience with health-care management. The doctor asks Jenny how she's doing, and Jenny speaks of her difficulty finding words and of the disappearance of some important documents. She mentions calling the police about a family she saw outside her house, because the parents were abusing their small children. The police came, but there was no one there when they arrived.

With Jenny's permission, Dr. T asks me and Barbara if we want to add anything. "You should know," I say, "that Jenny has loving friends and siblings in wide circles around her."

"That's good," says the doctor. Her voice is kind. She says she sees a change in Jenny from the first visit: more "hallucinations," more memory loss, more things going missing. "I see you have more trouble finding the words you want."

"Yes," says Jenny with a smile, "I have to be more poetic now."

All of a sudden I hear the doctor saying, "I believe you have Lewy Body dementia." I know this is a progressive dementia marked by hallucinations and delusions.

"Are you sure?" asks Barbara. It's the question of a loyal friend.

"About as sure as I can be," the doctor answers.

My stomach turns to stone. I look at Jenny, sitting silently on the edge of the examining table with her feet hanging over the side like a child's.

The doctor keeps going: "There's no definitive diagnosis of Lewy Body dementia, but the hallucinations, and the fact that Jenny is up and down, with both lucid days and confused days, are both typical signs of Lewy Body."

It's hard for me to take in the terrible meaning of what she is saying because it's so incongruous with her gentle voice.

Jenny is looking directly at the doctor. "What's going to happen to me?" she asks, right straight out. "How's it going to go?"

"It's going to get worse," the doctor says, "but I don't know how fast. It could take a while, but I'm afraid nothing can stop the downward spiral."

"What can I do about it?" She's doing what Buddhism teaches: don't turn away from what's difficult.

"There isn't really any treatment for it. But you can take care of your health and do the things you enjoy doing. It's also important for you and your loved ones to take steps now to plan for the future, before your judgment is seriously affected."

When we come out of the medical building into the sunshine, I feel like we're coming up from under water. Jenny is pale. Barbara says, "What do you want to do now, Jenny?" and Jenny responds without a pause, "I want a beer." We go to a German restaurant around the corner. The beer is good, but we're glum, and Jenny doesn't finish hers.

What do you say to a friend who has gotten such news? You have to say something. Barbara and I both promise Jenny we'll stick by her. I tell Jenny I think she's brave, the way she asked straightforward questions about what she wanted to know.

"I don't feel brave," says Jenny.

When the COVID-19 pandemic arrives, the order to shelter in place is especially hard on people living alone, like Jenny. In deference to safety guidelines, I don't go inside her apartment, though I'd like to visit and chat, or help her look for lost things. We can't go to the movies as we used to do quite often. Her neighborhood soup group has stopped meeting. As for Zoom meetings, a potential blessing during the pandemic, they are hard for Jenny to manage, what with lost passwords and other electronic devils.

I'm not her only friend, of course. As I told the doctor, Jenny has a circle of devoted friends, and that's not a coincidence, as she is a good and loyal friend herself. Her friends take walks with her, take her grocery shopping, help her with her computer, do errands with her and for her. Her neighbor across the hall is there night and day to help with lost keys, for reassurance, for plain old friendship. Jenny's devoted sister in Seattle manages bills and other pieces of Jenny's life from a distance, and she comes down from Seattle from time to time to work with Jenny on planning the next step. Jenny would do the same for all the people who are helping her.

As for me and Jenny, we keep on reading Buddhist books together. And in this strange pandemic time, the old-fashioned phone has been our link. Two afternoons a week, we read aloud to each other over the phone, alternating paragraphs, a few more pages each time. We experience each word of each book together, from start to finish.

For almost a year now, this reading aloud has been the path on which our friendship has continued. It's simple and focused. It's a devotional practice, and it takes concentration, especially for Jenny, because of her poor vision. With both eyes open, she sees double; even when she looks through her good eye only, the words jump around on the page.

She sometimes loses her place and repeats a line or skips a line, but she has been practicing patience for a long time, and one way or another, she always finds her way back in. At first, I had the impulse, when Jenny paused, to call out the next word, but I soon realized that that was an interruption of our practice together. I am glad to listen and wait until it's my turn. I'm moved by her perseverance. She doesn't get upset or apologize; she's reading not with her ego but out of devotion. The other day she told me that "it's hard to read because even after I see the words, it takes a little while for the meaning to come into the words."

It might look like I'm patient, too, but it doesn't take patience, because it doesn't matter to me how many pages we read in a day. The point is for me and Jenny to travel the text together. We are two old women kept apart by a pandemic, "sheltering in place," refuting the distance between us by reading religious texts aloud to each other over the phone.

———

We are reading Sharon Salzberg's classic text *Lovingkindness: The Revolutionary Art of Happiness*. Jenny reads an encouraging passage about how the practice of lovingkindness helps us to allow things to be the way they are.

I say to Jenny, "It might be easier for Sharon Salzberg to allow things to be the way they are than it is for you. She doesn't have Lewy Body. What do you think?"

"Things are okay right now," Jenny says.

———

Next, we go back a thousand years or so to an early Chinese Zen text, *The Platform Sutra: The Zen Teaching of Hui-neng*, with commentary by Red Pine. It's one of the most important sutras in Zen, and it's heartening and down-to-earth. We both appreciate the repeated instruction to practice with a straightforward mind. We are cheered by Hui-neng's refrain that we are all buddhas but we just don't know it. We all have the capacity for awakening.

It's my turn, and I come to the part where Hui-neng shouts out that even though we possess great wisdom, we can't understand this by ourselves. He tells us we need to find a true friend who can show us the way to our true nature.

I stop reading and declare, "That's us, my friend! We're showing each other the way."

"Yup," says Jenny. "We are."

———

After many weeks with *The Platform Sutra*, during which we do our best to have a straightforward mind, we turn to *The Art of Solitude*, the latest book by the Buddhist writer and teacher Stephen Batchelor. I hadn't heard about this book, but Jenny read a review of it and suggested it. She keeps up-to-date with Buddhist publishing. The book is a collage of Batchelor's explorations of solitude during his sixtieth year, through solo retreats, art, psychedelic drugs, and the writings of the French Renaissance philosopher Michel de Montaigne. We both love the book.

We are on the phone–she in her apartment, me in my house. Jenny is reading from Batchelor, who is telling us that we experience the great mystery of life whenever we are overwhelmed by the remarkable fact that we are here at all, rather than not here.

"Yes," I say to Jenny. "Isn't it amazing that we are here? We will *not* be here soon enough, but we're here now!"

Jenny excuses herself to get a drink of water, but she doesn't come back to the phone. I dimly hear her voice calling, "Sue! Where are you?" Across town from her, I shout into the receiver, "Jenny! Jenny! I'm on the *phone*!!!" I wait and shout again, but she doesn't hear me. I can't hear anything on the other end either, so I hang up. Five minutes later I call again. The phone rings and rings. Has the phone, a landline, come unplugged? Or could Jenny have fallen? Her balance isn't great. Worried, I make the twenty-minute drive over to her house in Oakland. When I pull up, she's standing on the corner outside, looking agitated. "Where *were* you?" she says. "Where did you go? I've been looking for you everywhere. I even went down to the basement. I came out to see if your car was still here."

I think for a fleeting moment of Stephen Batchelor and the great mystery that we are here at all, rather than not here. I say, "I wasn't here. We were talking on the phone."

"Oh no!" she says, suddenly realizing her mistake.

I don't go inside because of COVID. Instead, we collapse on a couple of chairs on the front porch and Jenny puts her head in her hands. Then she sits up and speaks in a voice of doom, "This is really bad. Really terrible. There's a protein in my head and it's eating holes in my brain."

Our next book is *The Heart Sutra*, translated and with commentary by Red Pine. I notice we've been unconsciously alternating ancient and modern texts. The *Heart Sutra*, a foundational text in Zen, is not a rational text. It reminds us that "form is emptiness and emptiness is form," that nothing is real and nothing is not real. It says, "There is no old age and death and also no extinction of old age and death." Red Pine takes the sutra one phrase at a time and gives extensive commentary, in a way that Jenny and I both experience as challenging, encouraging, and poetic. "I love doing this" Jenny says. "This is really good practice. When your mind wanders, you can bring it right back to the words you are reading."

The metaphysical nature of the *Heart Sutra* gives equal credence to Jenny's people in the trees and the people I see on the street, because it tells us they are all empty, all fleeting conjunctions of eyes and light and trees and everything we have "seen" and conceptualized in the past.

Red Pine tells us that what we call our eyes are "so many bubbles in a sea of foam."

We come to the mantra that closes the *Heart Sutra*: "*Gate, gate, paragate, parasamgate, bodhi svaha!*" Red Pine translates this as "Gone, gone, gone beyond, gone completely beyond. Enlightenment at last!"

Jenny reads, "The function of this mantra is to go beyond language . . ." She reads on, one word at a time, slow and steady. "And to lead us into the womb of Prajnaparamita, which is the Gone, the Gone Beyond, the Gone Completely Beyond."

"Wow!" she says. "He gives us the dharma upside the head! Let's read that again," and she does.

———

Jenny and I explore together what matters most to us. We have said this to each other: what a rare thing it is to have a friend with whom you can talk, without prelude, about your relationship with your beloved dead, or about time and how it passes, or about the difference between solitude and loneliness. We even talk about whether what we see is real.

———

We're reading the late Blanche Hartman's book of tiny dharma jewels, *Seeds for a Boundless Life*. In a piece called "Being Home," Jenny reads,

> Being at home wherever you are means being comfortable wherever you are. Not having to have some special place or special things to make you comfortable. Right here in this very body, in this very place as it is, is home.

"This is for you, Jenny," I say. "She's encouraging you for when you have to move. You can be at home anywhere."

"I know. My sleeping bag," she says.

"Your sleeping bag?"

"On the Camino, my home was my sleeping bag."

—

Another day I'm reading, "If we're open to embracing the surprises as they arise, then there will be inconceivable joy. If we fuss and fume and say, 'This isn't what I expected,' then there will be inconceivable misery." Hartman goes on, "Can you meet your life as it is and say, 'Just this is enough'?" I come to the end of the section and pause.

I'm thinking that it's all very well for me to say I accept my life just as it is, but it seems like a lot to ask of Jenny. I have more than enough of what I need, but Jenny is meeting loss after loss. At that moment she says, "I see these people in my house, and I don't want them sleeping in my bed. But I realize I have things they don't have. I should share with them."

—

Jenny didn't do anything to deserve Lewy Body—why did this happen to her? Sometimes, in a flash, I understand that it could just as easily be me. I want to remember this. I want to follow the counsel of the eighth-century Buddhist sage Shantideva and "make the exchange of self and other." I imagine myself in Jenny's shoes. We're not separate. *Lewy* and *Body* are two words, not a wall between us.

Still, I'm not going through what Jenny is going through. Her journey continues. She'll soon be leaving the home and neighborhood where she has lived for over thirty years, and this will be hard for her. Even as her confusion increases, as it is bound to do, her courage and forbearance will be valuable assets. We will continue to read Buddhist books together as long as we can, as long as it brings joy. I don't know what will happen, but I'll try to keep close.

Jenny's sister is helping her to find the next place that will be home, and wherever it is, we, her friends, will visit her.

Could I Be the Teacher
They Expected?

Magu, Nanquan, and another monk were on pilgrimage. Along the
way they met a woman who had a teashop by the side of the road.
The woman prepared a pot of tea and brought three cups. She said to
them, "Oh monks, let those of you with miraculous powers drink tea."

The three looked at each other, and the woman said, "Watch this
decrepit old woman show her own miraculous powers." Then she
poured tea into each cup and went out.

—ZEN KOAN FROM NINTH-CENTURY CHINA

I'VE COME TO love the old Zen stories. When my dharma sister
Florence Caplow and I compiled *The Hidden Lamp: Stories from
Twenty-Five Centuries of Awakened Women*, as mentioned earlier, my
affection for these stories grew. We gathered together one hundred stories, stories too-long neglected, about wise Buddhist women of the past–
nuns and abbesses, housewives and slaves, queens and prostitutes–and
paired each story with a commentary by a contemporary woman teacher.
I'm grateful to all these ancestors, generation beyond generation, and I
have a particular fondness for the nameless crones of ancient China, who
always seem to be hanging around by the side of the road, surprising Zen
monks on pilgrimage with their wisdom. One offers directions; another

has a tea shop, another serves rice cakes. These old women have gotten into my bones.

Six months after *The Hidden Lamp* was published, I received an email out of the blue: "I'm Koren, a nun of Zen Monastery Sanboji in Italy, near Parma. We would like to invite you in our Monastery. . . . We are interested at explorer koans about buddhist woman, your book is wonderful!" The monastery offered to pay my airfare to Italy.

I wear the green bib of a lay Zen teacher, and now and then I lead Zen retreats and classes, which I enjoy. At the time of the invitation, Florence and I were giving workshops and retreats based on *The Hidden Lamp* for American sanghas here and there, in places where we had connections or where the teacher was herself a contributor to *The Hidden Lamp*. But Italy?

I was past seventy, but in spite of my age, or perhaps because of it, I doubted the depth of my wisdom. I didn't like to call myself a "teacher"– a *Buddhist* teacher. It's not like teaching someone how to crochet. That's a skill I could transmit. But to fly all the way to Italy at the expense of an Italian temple in order to teach Buddhism to strangers–that would imply a sense of authority as a Zen teacher that I didn't feel I possessed. Besides, I don't speak Italian.

I had not heard of this place, but somehow they had heard of me. I didn't know whether Koren was Italian or Japanese, young or old. Later I learned that she was eager to bring forth women's teachings in her sangha, and when she heard about *The Hidden Lamp*, she invited me to Sanboji to teach, with the blessing of the center's founder and teacher, the Italian Zen master Tetsugen Serra Roshi. As for Sanboji, the temple itself, all I knew was what I found on Sanboji's website: a cloud of pink cherry blossoms in front of a white temple building with black roof tiles, and mountains–the Apennines–piled in layers behind it. I said yes.

More than a year later, I got off the plane in Milan feeling as if I had stepped off a hundred-foot pole, as the Zen saying goes. I went out through the security gate into a blast of heat—it was the hottest summer on record in Italy.

Two Italian monastics, a man and a woman, were waiting for me, easily recognizable by their black Zen clothing and the man's shaved head. The woman was holding flowers out to me. She hugged me as though I were her long-lost friend. She was Koren of the email, a youngish Italian woman with short dark hair and bright eyes; the man was Issan, a Spanish disciple of Master Tetsugen. She spoke very little English; he spoke a little more. I got into the car with these two strangers, who treated me as if I were exactly the beloved person they were expecting. But who *were* they expecting?

We drove for two and a half hours, out of the city, through fields dotted with round bales of hay, past rows of poplars, on roads that got smaller and bumpier, into the mountains, until finally we came down a long driveway to the monastery. We stepped through a big wrought iron gate. My guides led me past several old stone farm buildings, through a formal garden, and along a wooden walkway to a new building in the style of a traditional Zen temple.

We put our shoes on the shoe shelf, just as I do in California, and they ushered me into the daytime darkness of a large zendo that was shuttered against the heat of the sun. The main altar of a temple is the traditional first stop for a visitor. The smell of the tatami mats on the floor made me feel at home. A Zen temple smells like a Zen temple, in Japan, in Italy, or in California. Everything was familiar and everything was new.

"Do you want to offer incense?" Issan's question startled me. As a sign of respect, he was inviting me, the visiting teacher, to greet the temple before the retreat. I agreed. We approached the altar and he ceremoniously handed me a stick of incense. Nervous because I had never officially greeted a temple before, I started to put the incense into the wrong bowl. Issan's hand appeared before me, pointing to the bowl in front of Buddha. He stepped back silently as I planted the stick in the ashes. Everything was fine. There was nothing in the room but kindness– it lapped around me as I made my three full bows.

Koren led me to the visiting teacher's quarters. Inside, I was greeted by an impressive scroll: a red-robed Bodhidharma peered out at the spacious room from under his heavy eyebrows. My futon bed floated in the middle of a wide tatami sea, with two brightly colored paper cranes perched on my pillow. In an alcove, an altar with a vase of blue cornflowers. On a low table, a bowl of strawberries.

After Koren left, I opened one of the big casement windows and swung back the shutters to a view of faraway mountains and nearby, more blue cornflowers. My bare feet liked the tatami. I felt like a traveler in an old children's book who had passed through a turnstile into an enchanted realm. Restless with a mixture of happiness and anxiety– *Was it really me, here?*–I walked around the room and paused in front of Bodhidharma. I sat on a little stool and faced him.

He looked at me with his penetrating, lidless gaze, and, because he was the only person at Sanboji who was familiar to me, I asked him for help. "Here *you* are!" I said out loud. "Thanks for bringing Buddhism from India to China so long ago. And now you've come all the way to Italy!" I was crying, but not with grief. "Who do they think I am? Am I the wrong person?"

I seemed to hear Bodhidharma reply: *You've studied Buddhism for almost forty years. You know me. You've explored the teachings and you've shared the teachings. You've given your life, in your own way, to* this *way. Where else should you be but here?* When he said that, I felt my life of practice flowing through me like blood, making my hands and feet tingle.

The dinner bell rang, and as I stood up, Bodhidharma added, *You can do this.*

The next morning, I went for a walk along a ridge, past hayfields, and took a turn where a sign said PAGAZZANO. The neighboring village appeared before me, a cluster of red tile roofs in tiers on a hill, with the church steeple rising up in the middle. As I entered the village, I had the feeling of passing through another gate, into yet another world. I thought of the Zen vow that says, "Dharma gates are boundless; I vow to enter them." My world, the Sanboji world, and now the world of Pagazzano—three completely different worlds, one gate after another.

I followed a narrow, cobbled street up the hill, between gray stone houses, many of them crumbling into rock piles. A few, standing wall to wall between the ruins, sported bright window boxes of well-watered geraniums, splashes of red on the gray stone. Some chickens were clucking in a fenced yard. It felt spooky, this cobblestone ghost town. Who was feeding the chickens? Who was watering the geraniums?

I continued up the street until I came upon the church and a little plaza with a fountain, and there at last was a live human being—an old man sitting on the wall.

"*Buongiorno, signore,*" I said, using up about half of my Italian vocabulary, and he answered me in a stream of cheerful Italian.

I asked with gestures if I could go into the church, and he indicated it was locked. He disappeared up the street and returned almost immediately with an old woman, wiry and upright, whose bright blue eyes matched her blue dress. She unlocked the door and led me into the cool arched space that smelled of stone.

Another old woman followed us in—an "American," the first old woman said by way of introduction—and she spoke to me in fluent but accented English. She said she had been born in Pagazzano and had lived in New York as a young woman. Now, in her flowered housedress, she looked as though she had never left Pagazzano, except for her dyed red hair. She told me she was ninety-one years old and the woman with the key was ninety.

The church looked clean and cared for, though the lilies on the altar were plastic. I asked whether there were services on Sundays. No, the "American" said, only on Christmas, Easter, and special occasions like weddings.

"How many people live in Pagazzano?" I asked.

She conferred with the woman in blue. "About fifty, now, in the summer," she said.

"How many live here all year round?"

Another conference, more subdued this time. "Eight," she said.

"*Eight*?"

She nodded, blushing as if embarrassed for her village.

I felt like an exchange student coming from the present to visit the past. I'd been in Pagazzano half an hour and already I had met a large proportion of the population: the man at the fountain and these two women, all of them erect and energetic, living on and on as the walls collapsed around them. I wanted to cry for the village and its unused church with the plastic flowers. I couldn't imagine what it would be like to be an old woman living in the dream that was Pagazzano.

That afternoon the curtain went up at Sanboji. About thirty students arrived, along with Gabriella, my professional translator. Half the participants were men, which was unusual for a *Hidden Lamp* retreat, and many of them were young. Their energy was fresh. Everyone, men and women, old and young, sat before me on their cushions and looked at me attentively as I spoke.

I asked them, via Gabriella's translation, to talk in pairs about an old woman who had nurtured them in their own lives—a grandmother, aunt, or teacher. I watched them become more animated as they warmed to the topic. Back in the large group, they shared what they had discovered while Gabriella, sitting next to me, whispered her simultaneous translation in my ear. "I never realized before how important my grandma was to me—she always gave me a bowl of hot chocolate when I came home from school." I was especially touched by the openness of the young men, who spoke in their resonant voices of the old women who had loved them when they were boys.

During the weekend we studied several koans in depth, including "The Old Woman's Miraculous Powers," the one about the tea-shop keeper who demonstrates her miraculous powers by pouring tea for three monks on pilgrimage.

We talked about miracles. Not levitating, not passing through walls, but taking the dog for a walk or offering chunks of Parmesan cheese to a visitor. I asked them to tell each other, in pairs, their own miraculous powers. I don't know what they said, but they looked engrossed.

When you're at home and everything is familiar, it's hard to remember how miraculous everything is. When you go to a new place, everything freshens up. I was far from home. I, too, was freshened up. I was sitting in the teacher's seat, breathing, laughing, and still wondering, *Was this really* me—*this woman Sanboji had brought forth?* It was a me I hardly trusted, but a me the Italians didn't doubt.

I divided people into small groups and asked each group to prepare a skit based on a different koan from the book. In the United States, this exercise has sometimes fallen flat, when people have felt shy. Not so for the Italians! There was wailing and gnashing of teeth, operatic singing, wild dancing, raucous laughter. Interpretive liberties were taken, and that was fine with me. A handsome young man played the part of an old woman by the side of the road who directed pilgrims to Mount Wutai. "Right straight ahead," she always said, sometimes pointing one way, sometimes another. Koren, my hostess, played an old woman bent over her cane, weeping over the death of her granddaughter. When three monks made fun of her tears, she suddenly stood up straight, gave a martial shout, and knocked them to the ground with her cane, using elegant karate-like moves, in an Italian embellishment to the original koan. I didn't need Gabriella to translate anything for me. Each performance brought down the house. Here, at Sanboji, the old stories were coming alive.

Before breakfast, on the last day of the retreat, Koren led us out through the monastery gate and up the road in silent walking meditation. I hung back to walk at the end of the line, the better to enjoy the vision of thirty monks in single file moving through the hayfields, as one organism. Then Koren turned up the cobbled street into Pagazzano, the same street I had taken a few days before.

There was nobody about as our silent line moved up the hill. We were hot and thirsty by the time we got to the fountain by the church, and, following Koren's example, we broke ranks and drank from the spout.

When I straightened up, I saw the old woman who kept the church key. There, suddenly, was the brightness of her white hair, of her blue eyes. She was holding a pail of water with a rag hanging over the rim. She must have been about to wash the church steps.

She surprised me, just as people in Zen koans do; she seemed to have materialized out of thin air, smiling. She, on the other hand, seemed not at all surprised to meet thirty Zen monks at the fountain. She recognized me and gave me a hug, proving herself to be made of solid flesh. Koren greeted her, and they talked and laughed together. So Koren knew her! I was startled to find that the worlds of Sanboji and Pagazzano were acquainted. They seemed to me to occupy two different universes, even though they were only about a mile apart. "What is the old woman saying?" I asked Issan, who was standing beside me.

He grinned. "She invited all of us to come and live with her in Pagazzano, to keep her company."

Koren said goodbye and we returned to single file. As we made our way down the cobbled street in silence, I thought about the old woman washing the steps of the church that didn't hold services anymore, watering the geraniums, greeting whoever came along. She was taking care of her dying village, completely cheerful.

All of a sudden it came to me: I had met the Old Woman by the Side of the Road. The quintessential old woman in the koans, the one pouring tea and giving directions to Mount Wutai, was here right now.

She was an Italian woman in a blue housedress who had stepped through time while fetching water at the fountain. We monks had stopped for refreshment along the way, and there she was, water pail in hand, a visitation, come to encourage us. She was the Old Woman of Pagazzano.

All the way back to the monastery my heart was pounding with joy. *The Old Woman is here right now! The Old Woman is here right now!* From Pagazzano to Sanboji, the fields beside the road shimmered in the heat of the sun.

When we gathered in the zendo after breakfast, I was bursting with excitement. I said to the students, "A miracle happened this morning! Do you know what it was?" I imagined a chorus of voices would call out, "The Old Woman of Pagazzano!" But they looked at me with puzzled faces. How could they all have missed it?

"We met the wise Old Woman from ancient China," I said. "Remember? At the fountain? Ninth-century China and twenty-first-century Pagazzano are the same place! The women in *The Hidden Lamp* are not dead. Their stories are not covered with dust."

They saw it then and nodded happily. Perhaps they, too, had had significant meetings during their weekend retreat in the Apennines–meetings unknown to me.

The retreat ended and Sanboji emptied out again. The students went home, but I stayed on for an extra day and Issan took me back to the village of Pagazzano for a special event: the cardinal of Parma was making his biannual visit. This time, about two dozen people were assembled, and the lilies were the kind that filled the church with fragrance. Issan whispered a translation in my ear as the cardinal gave a short talk about how the faith in Italy was still strong. When he finished, he invited questions. The Old Woman of Pagazzano observed that churches all around Italy were closing, and she asked if he would ever close this church. He said never, *never*, because the village took very good care of the church and it was the cleanest in the region. This made me think it could be the old woman herself, with her water bucket and scrub rag, who was keeping the church alive.

Afterward, in the café next door, the village women passed around trays of homemade pastries. My blue-eyed friend poured prosecco for anyone who wanted it, including the cardinal, who sat informally at a big slab table with some of the local men. I watched her. She could have been pouring tea for monks on pilgrimage. She could have said, "Watch this decrepit old woman show her own miraculous powers."

She sat down and tapped the space on the bench beside her, looking at me. I sat too, and we smiled and nodded at each other. I pointed at myself: "Susan"; and she pointed at herself: "Maria." She was my host, I was her guest—as intimate as two palms pressed together, in a bow or a prayer.

To find myself a welcome guest at the village party, drinking prosecco with the cardinal of Parma—what a conflation of worlds, and what proof that all those worlds were one.

I was not quite yet an old woman by the side of the road, myself; I was old, yes, but I was still *on* the road. My road went right through Pagazzano, and the blue-eyed woman was there, like a mirror, urging me to show my own miraculous powers.

Going and Coming

MY TEACHER IS dying. My first, my old, Zen teacher. His wife, Liz, who has become my friend over the years, ushers me into their comfy house. Mel is in a hospital bed in the dining room, propped up at an angle, facing out the west windows of the house toward San Francisco Bay. He's called Sojun, or Sojun Roshi, in a formal Zen setting, but in this moment he's Mel. I sit down in the chair that waits for me, next to his bed. He wears a nasal cannula, its plastic tubes crossing his face to deliver oxygen to his nostrils. I wear a flowered cotton mask on account of the coronavirus. I identify myself, unsure whether the mask makes me unrecognizable, and he responds with an enthusiastic "Aah," a simple vowel sound that connects us. He seems glad to see me.

I'm shocked by his appearance. His mouth is wide open, in a perfect O. He's so gaunt that his body barely makes a mound under the light quilt. His face is thinner, too. At the same time, I know him, the person who introduced me to Zen practice almost fifty years ago. I make sentences in my mind: *I can see death in him. His open mouth is like an* enso—*a Zen circle.* These are some of the thoughts I think, and even while I'm thinking them, I know I am making them up. What do these thoughts have to do with the person I love who is right in front of me, breathing?

Since he went into hospice care a couple of weeks ago, sangha members have been coming to see him. There are so many people who want to visit him–people more involved than I with the daily nitty-gritty of the Zen center–that I didn't expect to have this chance to say goodbye. But because I've known him for such a long time, I have been given the gift of half an hour to sit with him.

The sun has just come low enough to shine directly into his eyes through the uncurtained window. Liz raises up the hospital tray table, swivels it across the bed, and hangs a cloth napkin from it to shade his face. Her movements are at once tender and practical. "How's that?" she asks.

He gives a slight nod and murmurs a barely audible, "Better."

She strokes his forehead and says she's leaving us to ourselves; she has a project to work on.

"What's your project?" I ask.

"Setting rat traps in the basement," she tells me with a rueful shrug and leaves the room.

I tell him I'm glad to see him. He seems to be listening but doesn't say anything back. I talk about how long I've known him, how much he means to me, how grateful I am for his teaching. "You always taught us to take care of what's in front of us." I feel awkward making these straightforward declarations, without nuance, without humor, and without a clear response, but I keep going. "You told me it's okay for me to be me." I'm glad Liz has left the room–I might be too self-conscious to say such things if she were still there, though I doubt that she would mind. I say, "You've had a long, full life."

Now I hear him speaking. I lean closer and I hear the word *voyage*.

"Yes, it's a big voyage," I say, not sure if he means his life or his dying. Maybe both.

I'm flooded with appreciation. Perhaps I should just sit still with him. After all, that's what he's been teaching me to do all these years–to sit in silence. Yes, I will do that, but first I want to speak some more, because it makes me feel connected. The sound of my voice is an offering I make to him. I talk briefly of memories of the early days of the Zen center he started, including how, after Monday morning zazen, Liz would make a hearty breakfast, usually oatmeal, for anyone who wanted to stay. How he taught us during work period to wash the leaves of the big rubber plant in the living room with milk. Then I worry: maybe he's not interested in my anecdotes of long ago–why would he be? He's doing the work of this moment. He's interested in what's happening at this very moment.

I stop talking and we sit in silence. He's alive. Soon he will be gone, but we're here now, in the same room, in the same late afternoon. His dying is a shock, not to my reason, because he's had cancer for a year and a half and he's ninety-one; I've known for months that his death is coming soon. But now that I see with my eyes that he's going to die, it's a shock to my whole system, like a big change in the weather.

It used to seem that he would never die, because he was always there, somewhere near at hand, strong and steady, hardly aging, riding his bicycle in the early morning across town to the zendo; or in his office at the Zen center, available to whoever knocked; or glimpsed out my living room window walking his dog on my block; or most essentially, on his amazingly thin cushion in the zendo, in full lotus, every morning.

Year after year, he stood at the door of the zendo as we filed out after morning service, and he looked each of us in the eye and we bowed to each other. As I stood in line to go out, I looked forward to that moment of seeing and being seen. It was the best eye contact you could ask for.

Now I sit still with him as the world shifts.

Once, in the beginning days of my practice, a handful of us were sitting in the old attic zendo for early morning zazen, under Mel's caring attention, and an earthquake shook the floorboards beneath us. The eaves in front of our faces shifted and the redwood rafters creaked. It was over almost as soon as I realized what it was, and we were returned to silence. I was scared, but nobody moved or spoke, and my fear turned into wonder that I had received this earthquake without moving, that I had made the passage from one side of it to the other, from silence to silence.

Mel keeps moistening his lips with his tongue. I call to Liz, "He seems thirsty," and she comes from the kitchen–she must be finished with the rat traps. She holds a small cup of water to his lips, tips it carefully for a couple of sips, then goes away again. Mel is alive, drinking water. It's so simple. I read him a short poem I picked out ahead of time by Zen Master Dogen.

> Water birds
> going and coming
> their traces disappear
> but they never
> forget their path.

I ask if he wants to hear another, but I can't tell whether the answer is yes or no, so I read a few more poems, until it feels like time to stop.

Time passes strangely, neither fast nor slow. We sit quietly. His hand lies palm down on the cover at the near edge of the bed, in easy reach of my hand. I long to put my palm on the back of his hand and wrist–the skin looks so soft–but, remembering the virus, I don't. I wonder to myself if I would do it if the virus didn't stop me.

The last of the sunlight is golden on the redwood paneling of the walls. Then the sun itself sinks behind a rooftop across the street, and Mel gestures toward the now unnecessary cloth napkin. I remove it. The sky is bright pink, sending a wash of pink into the room.

"It's nice that you can be here at home, in this beautiful room," I say, "with Liz taking such good care of you." Now he is talking, and I lean in again. His voice is very quiet, with little breath to spare, and his mouth is dry and wants to stay open, so it's hard for him to enunciate. But I hear him say, "Yes, it's a nice house." Perhaps he says so to be kind, to make the sort of conversation with me that I seem to want.

Liz comes into the living room. I say, "I know, it's time for me to go." Mel makes a scooping motion with an arm that seems to suggest: *You can stay a little longer.* I'm touched, but I say, to reassure Liz, "My half hour is up."

She says, "It's just that it's important not to tire him."

What does it mean to say goodbye? It comes to me that I'm telling myself a story, and the story goes: *My Zen teacher is dying and I'm saying goodbye. I've known him almost fifty years, and he has always encouraged me to be myself. He did his best to teach me that I have everything I need. Now he's dying and will soon be gone. These are his last days. This is an important moment because it's the last time I will ever see him.*

There's nothing wrong with stories. I'm telling you one right now, and inside this written story is the story I was telling myself as I sat beside my teacher's hospital bed. But he wasn't telling himself this story. He was breathing, going from one breath to the next one.

I stand up and say, "Goodbye. I love you." I put my hands together and give him a little bow.

He says, distinctly, "Goodbye," and he lifts his hands from the bedcover and looks me in the eye and bows back.

That's what really happened. I'm making it into a story now by telling you about it after it happened. But while it was happening it wasn't a story yet. It wasn't inside my head, like thoughts, it was simply what our bodies did.

Note: Sojun Mel Weitsman, founder, abbot, and guiding teacher of Berkeley Zen Center, died ten days after this meeting, on January 6, 2021, at the age of ninety-one.

If I Can Still Love

IT'S HARD TO get old. Some things get easier the longer you practice them, like parking the car or peeling a potato, but not getting old, because the longer you do it, the older you get. There are losses, big and small—of physical strength, of proper nouns, of a sense of direction, of keys and reading glasses, of bowel regularity, of your driver's license, of hearing, of loved ones. Some of us lose more than others, but everyone loses something. Everything keeps changing, as Buddha repeatedly pointed out, and just when you've adapted to one loss, you can get sideswiped by another. You don't know what's going to happen next.

But impermanence is good news, too. Occasionally things change for the better. Even if you're old and getting older, you can't assume that tomorrow will be worse than today. Something wonderful might happen quite unexpectedly, or you might collaborate with reality to make something wonderful happen. You might take a walk in Tilden Park, in the hills behind Berkeley, and see the first bluebirds you've ever seen in your life, a whole flock of them, out of the blue, flying over a field. This happened to my sister a week ago, and she's getting old.

Each morning, you wake up into an unused day, neither wilted nor dented. We talk about this in the Crones Group I'm part of, about how an old person's life can still be a fresh life. So keep that in mind. Stop and think about what you enjoy and what you can do well, like trying out a new soup recipe, crocheting a scarf for a friend who lives in a cold place, looking at a person you care about and noticing how particularly themselves they are, or taking a walk in the evening light.

What is it, this oldness? I turn first to the downside.

In my sixties, I wrote a book about getting old, and now, in my seventies, I understand that I was still quite young back then. I feel more compassion now for very old people than when I wasn't in the club. I think of my late mother and feel sorry that I wasn't more sympathetic toward her when I was a youth in my fifties and sixties.

I recall how much her back hurt her in the short walk from her apartment to the elevator; of her frustration with her computer, and how mad she got when she couldn't remember how to set the margins on her documents. She wrote poetry, and margins are especially important for poetry because they affect the line breaks. We worked on her margins every time I visited her, but most of the time I was far away, and trying to help her on the phone made us both irritable. It must have been hard to be a poet who had lost control over her margins. After she died, I wished I had been more able to show her the keen love I felt for her. My tendency to regress in her presence to the monosyllabic conversation style of a teenager, a sixty-five-year-old teenager, held me back. *I'm sorry, Mom. I loved you, but I didn't realize what you were up against–the aches and pains and Swiss cheese brain. Now I'm an old woman, just like you, and I still love you. Can you hear me?*

Now that my own aging is teaching me more empathy for old folks than I had for my mother, I encourage you to learn this lesson earlier than I did, before all the people you want to be empathetic to are dead. By the way, I'm not addressing my own grown children here. They are as caring to me as I could wish.

It may feel prudent in our society to hide the physical signs of aging and to bluff our way through our mental losses. The frailties of age are seen as shameful or, at best, the stuff of pitiful jokes on birthday cards. An old woman in a long purple dress announces, "There are a lot of advantages to being old . . . you can laugh, cough, sneeze, and pee at the same time." I guess such a card is funny when one old person sends it to another. My old, old friends (my elderly, longtime friends) and I often complain to each other about worsening knees and memories, but I notice that in conversation with younger people, I try to keep a stiff upper lip.

I want to speak of what's actually happening, not to make you laugh or persuade you to feel sorry for me. I'm looking for a path of dignity, somewhere between bluffing and whining, a straightforward path of *This is how it is right now.*

As I come out of the closet about my losses, especially the cognitive ones, I risk being condescended to or even dismissed. But there are others who struggle with problems similar to mine and who feel alone, particularly in connection with their cognitive decline. It's scary and hard to talk about. So I'm going to talk about it.

My Buddhist practice helps me here, reminding me not to turn away from what's difficult. And I have noticed that when I speak about my experience straightforwardly, people are surprisingly interested and respectful.

Besides, it's not all bad. There are wonderful things about getting old that have nothing to do with peeing and sneezing. I'll come to that. I'm saving the best for last.

But first, paying attention to the losses, I've come up with four practices to aid the aging.

1. *Observe.* This is how it is right now.
2. *Adapt.* Do it differently from the way you used to do it.

3. *Let Go.* If you can't find a way to do it differently, let it go altogether.

4. *Accept.* This is how it is right now. Like I said.

I'll take these one at a time.

Observe

I'm fortunate to be in good physical health for the time being. I can't do handstands anymore, but I can chew, swallow, digest, and eliminate–four simple things I used to take for granted. Sometimes my swallowing doesn't go completely smoothly, which is scary, and sometimes there are glitches with the elimination part, but generally I can get things both in and out.

I no longer take for granted my ability to walk and talk, to see and hear. I have friends who can't do some of these things. Seven years ago I couldn't walk very well myself, due to painful arthritis in my knees. I had both knees replaced and now they serve me well. So, gratitude is in order.

My cognitive functioning is another story, and that's what I want to focus on here. I'm trying to notice *with* my mind what's happening *to* my mind, while I still can. I want to bear witness to my own decline. Dispassionately. Wait, I'm going to dispense with the word *decline*. I'm going to bear witness to the *changes* in my mind.

My vocabulary is shrinking rapidly. What's that word for forgetting words? That's what I have. Buddha said that wise speech has three qualities: it should be true, it should be beneficial, and it should be said at the right time. He forgot to mention a fourth requirement: you need to have the words for what you want to say.

There's nothing new for me about forgetting proper names, but now they are leaving in droves. Worse yet, the rude common nouns are joining the proper ones in the exodus. I may have an interesting anecdote to add to the conversation, but sometimes I don't say anything because I can't remember the words I need to tell the story.

Just the other day, I couldn't think of the word for skylight. *Skylight???!!!* I was standing in the attic with the contractor, pointing helplessly at a place in the roof. "How soon will the . . ." He seamlessly filled in the word for me, and blushing, I finished with "be installed?"

I'm a writer, and it seems that the tools of my trade are being taken from me. Why is this happening? Is it my fault for cooking with aluminum pots? I'm worried. Can I be dignified and forgetful at the same time? Putting these anxious questions aside, I come back to the practice of observing: this is how it is right now.

Sometimes a wrong word comes out of my mouth that doesn't belong in the sentence at all. I say *tablecloth* instead of *bedspread, onion* instead of *lemon.*

I get times and dates mixed up, showing up for a Thursday meeting on Tuesday, because Tuesday and Thursday seem like twins.

My once excellent sense of direction is shaky. I can't find my way to places I used to know. Did that knitting store close or is it actually on another street? I can't look up the address because I forget the name of the store.

I get turned around easily, and when I come out on the street from the subway, or out of the restroom in a big medical office building, I turn the wrong direction as often as not. I might find myself in an empty banquet room or looking at water instead of land. It's disorienting, as if a helicopter has deposited me blindfolded, not only into an unmapped place but into an unmetered time. It is indeed an unknown time, this time of my life. I haven't been in it before.

My short-term memory is getting even shorter. Sometimes, when a friend is telling me an important story about her life, I forget who the pronouns refer to, just a few minutes into the narrative. She says, "I couldn't believe that he did it again!" and the bottom drops out of my mental bucket. *Who is she talking about? What was it he did?* I was listening, but I've already lost the thread. *Should I ask?*

Even as I revise this essay, I have to keep looking back to see if I already said something I meant to say. Have I included the paragraph about love or have I moved it to the end?

Bearing witness is another way to say observing. Bearing witness includes honoring the loss and grieving it. I encourage myself to make space for the loss; make space for the grief. Say goodbye to the word *skylight*. Let the word fly up through the hole in the roof into the open sky. Say goodbye to the map that used to be in my head, goodbye to knowing where everything is, including the knitting store, and say goodbye to needing to know everything I used to know.

Adapt

Adaptation is key to aging. As one of the Tibetan mind-training slogans says, "Turn all difficulties into the path."

My siblings and I persuaded our mother to stop driving when she was about eighty. She liked to be out and about, and this was a terrible loss for her. She got upset with us, and now I think it was not just because she had to stop driving but because we didn't understand how great the deprivation was.

"You can take the bus," I said.

"No, I *can't*! It hurts my back to walk to the bus stop!"

Oh, right. I'd forgotten that her back hurt after walking just one block. "Well, you can take a cab," I suggested.

"It takes *forever* to get a cab here!" she said, with tears in her voice.

Then she discovered that the senior housing facility where she lived had one of those motorized scooter chairs available for residents, and she learned to take herself to the bus stop, get on an accessible bus, ride to downtown Chicago, and take the scooter to a concert or poetry reading without having to worry about parking. She was proud of having figured out this way to be independent. It was a triumph. She had turned a difficulty into the path—the path of the mobility scooter.

As for myself, I'm making a number of adaptations. Take my shrinking vocabulary, for example. When I'm writing, I make frequent use of the thesaurus as I search for a forgotten word. In this way I remind myself of all sorts of other words, often more interesting than the one I was looking for. When I'm talking, it's not feasible to interrupt the conversation while I search the thesaurus on my cell phone, so I use short words. I learned the short words first, and the first words learned are the last to go, so they are still in my head. Hey, look at that last sentence—all one-syllable words! English is a great language for one-syllable words. It's time to speak and write more simply now, and perhaps more freshly. It's also a good time to listen more and talk less.

Here's a very practical adaptation that I'm proud of. I enjoy cooking, but I can't hold the list of ingredients in my head. I find myself checking the recipe repeatedly, interrupting the flow and taking the time to fetch each ingredient as I go along. I've had the melting butter burn while I was looking for the can of diced chiles.

I'm pleased with my solution. Before I start cooking, I go down the list of ingredients and bring each one to the counter, along with whatever measuring cups, spoons, whisks, knives, or bowls I'll need. I line up the cast on the kitchen counter in order of appearance, and I'm ready to begin.

I have instituted some further protocols: I try to have only one pot on the heat at a time, and I don't listen to audiobooks or talk radio or even songs with words, unless they are in a foreign language I don't understand. Only instrumental music is allowed while cooking, lest I put in a tablespoon of salt instead of a teaspoon.

As for mixing up times and dates, an obvious adaptation for me would be to simplify my life so that I don't have to keep track of so many appointments. If the things I do are things I love to do, then I should give the doing of them full due. I've been talking about simplifying my life for years, but it will take being brutally honest with myself and admitting that I can't fit everything in that I used to fit in. Simplifying my life brings me straight to the third step.

Let Go

Sometimes there isn't a good adaptation. Sometimes you can't find a new way to do something that you used to do easily and you just have to stop doing it. You have to let it go.

The Theravadan Buddhist teacher Ajahn Sumedho likes to say, "The essence of Buddhism, in six words, is 'Let go, let go, let go.'" It's the essence of aging, too. Hey, I just noticed: "getting old" sort of rhymes with "letting go." It's an anagram, except that the *d* in *old* is extra.

I've let go of driving alone at night because I get sleepy. I've let go of riding a bicycle because my balance isn't great. I'm trying to let go of doing more than one big thing in a day, e.g., don't have cataract surgery and then go to a birthday party.

I have trouble simplifying my life because I want to do what I want to do. I'm greedy. I want to teach and write and read the books in a pile by my bed and visit my faraway grandchildren. I want to go to all-day Zen retreats, work on election campaigns, go to the movies, make dinner for friends, and help my sister hem the kitchen curtains.

Zen practice reminds me that I can't be in more than one place at a time. But I can't even be in *one* place at a time when I leave myself no transition time. It takes me longer now to shift my attention from one activity to another. I need quiet so I can focus, and I'm going to have to give some things up, including things I love to do–that's all there is to it. But which ones?!?

My late friend Maylie Scott gave me some good advice long ago: "The secret is to regulate your life." She was busy, though the word *busy* trivializes what she did. She shared her big old Berkeley house with others and led a full life as a Zen teacher, peace activist, caregiver, writer, mother, and grandmother. In spite of her many interests and community responsibilities, she always seemed to move deliberately. She showed up on time, she led and encouraged and cared. She told me once that the way she kept from getting overcommitted and overwhelmed was by going to Berkeley Zen Center for 5:40 a.m. and 5:40 p.m. zazen every day. She said, "You'd think that taking so much time for practice would make it harder to get everything done, but on the contrary, my other activities fall into place around zazen, and the things that aren't important have to fall away."

Slow down, quiet down, settle down.

Letting go can be positive. You can use getting old as the excuse for not doing the things that you really don't want to do anymore anyway–serving on certain committees, for example. There are also the internal things I'm eager to let go of, like old grudges, self-blame, and regrets. Releasing regrets is an appropriate practice for us older people. As I look back over my life, I realize that I can't change what I already did, and it's mostly too late to make amends in any literal way. But there's no need to carry these burdensome regrets to the very edge of the grave. I'm learning to acknowledge a mistake and then let the wind take it. I'd like to give myself the gift of dying without regrets.

A close friend and dharma sister died recently, of cancer, and I hadn't said goodbye to her. Susan lived an hour's drive away, and I visited her many times during the last year of her life, but I hadn't seen her for a couple of months before she died. Many people loved her, and sometimes more people wanted to visit her than she had the energy for. I told myself she would email me if she wanted me to come. I didn't want to bother her, but she might not have wanted to bother me, either. I thought she was stable, but she went very fast at the end. I was far away on a trip when she went into the hospital and entered palliative care. She died in a matter of days.

I'm heartbroken at the loss of a dear friend. The painful grief takes away my appetite. It breaks me wide open with love. It sometimes disables me, but I want to feel it. The extra part that I don't want to feel is the twist of regret like a rusty corkscrew down my throat. I blame myself for not staying in close enough touch to say goodbye, not telling her I loved her before she died. I berate myself: *What were you thinking? If you had been a true friend, you wouldn't have held back!*

I know Susan wouldn't want me to feel this. I imagine her supporting me now, just as she did when she was alive. So here is the practice I've made for myself. Each time I'm seized by this burning regret, I take a deep breath, I close my hands into loose fists, and as I exhale, I open my palms slowly and say softly, "I love you, Susan." (Just to be clear, I'm *not* talking to myself.) I'm learning that loosening my hold on a particular regret may not happen in one fell swoop, but if I keep on opening my closed hands, over and over, metaphorically as well as literally, letting go becomes possible.

Accept

Sometimes the difficulty doesn't lend itself to letting go. Your back hurts when you wake up. The pain won't let go of you, and you can't let go of the pain.

That's when you get to the bottom line. There is still something left to let go of and that's the idea that things should be different. I've heard more than one Buddhist teacher say that our biggest problem is that we think we shouldn't have a problem. If you can let go of wanting the moment to be otherwise, you can get your life back. I tell myself, *This is how it is right now.*

It was Susan who gave me that sentence—something to hold like a smooth stone in my pocket. I was visiting her while she was undergoing aggressive chemotherapy, and she was feeling exhausted and nauseous.

She told me that she would tell herself: "This is how it is right now." She said it calmly. She wasn't trying to be someone else, somewhere else, in some other time.

One of the most difficult things to accept is the fact of my own cognitive decline. At my request, my doctor sent me to a neurologist for a screening. I had gone to a psychologist ten years earlier out of the same concern and had been told that I was "doing very well *for my age*" [emphasis mine]. This time it was a neurologist, not a psychologist, and he surprised me with the physical components of the test. As well as asking me to identify a picture of a rhinoceros and some other objects, he tapped my knees with that little rubber hammer. Luckily, my memory was still good enough that I remembered to kick. Passing his test didn't inspire my confidence, but he assured me that I am in the normal range for my age. Without getting personal, he added that the range is very wide and includes some cognitive decline. So, yes, I know it's happening, and I might as well accept the new normal. Isn't it sort of strange that what's normal doesn't stay the same? I used to think that was the whole point of normal. It should be reliable. At any rate, the visit alleviated my anxiety, which was helpful. Someday I might go for cognitive testing and it might not be "normal." Then I'll have something really hard to accept–all the more reason for practicing acceptance now.

Clay is an old friend from Berkeley Zen Center who suffers from severe chronic back pain that began twenty years ago when he was in his thirties. I remember when he started lying down on the zendo floor for zazen. He's not old, but his story offers encouragement for anyone dealing with chronic pain, and that is often a part of aging. Clay came over to my house recently to talk about a writing project, and at first he sat in a folding reclining chair he takes with him wherever he goes, until the pain caught up with him in that position. Then he lay on his back on the floor on top of an ice pack, and we continued to talk. His situation is like aging speeded up and amplified.

Some years after its original onset, the pain got even worse due to a herniated disk in Clay's neck, and he had to give up an important work project he had just begun. He told me, "I would meditate at home while lying down, and the waves of grief and despair just washed through me. The tears would run down my cheeks and collect in my ears so that when I sat up, they would spill out onto my shirt." He let the tears come, and they washed him and nourished him. "After a while," he said, "I found myself crying not so much about my own state as about other things, like news reports that were sad, or beautiful trees and flowers—just things that really touched my heart."

Finally, a doctor told him there was nothing medicine could do for him beyond helping him with pain management. "You can't ever expect to go back to a regular job. Your job from now on is to take care of yourself." Clay said at first he was crushed and then he was relieved. He felt *This is my life. I accept it.*

Clay says, "I'm fifty-five years old and my condition has gradually worsened with age. However, my ability to find joy in my life has actually increased, despite the worsening of my condition."

A line from Hakuin's "Song of Zazen" says, "Truly is anything missing now?"

The practice of accepting includes accepting help.

After my double knee replacements when I was seventy, I was sent to a rehab facility for a week. I was fortunate to be there; the nursing assistants, in spite of being overworked, attended to me kindly, and the physical therapy was excellent. But the pain in my legs was severe, and the meds made me dizzy and nauseous. I had trouble eating, sleeping, and eliminating. Every night I soaked the bed with sweat. I tried, with limited success, to focus on my breathing, on getting through each moment one breath at a time. Several times a day, a woman down the hall wailed her refrain, over and over, with the desperation of a person hanging from the edge of a cliff: "Help me! Help me! Where's my nurse? Help me! Now! Now!" I asked one of the nurses why no one was helping her, and she tapped herself on the head and said, "We stopped trying, because when we go to her, she doesn't need anything. She wants someone to talk to, and we don't have time to sit there with her." Still, I felt like the woman was calling out to Kuan Yin, the bodhisattva of compassion who hears the cries of the world; she was voicing the pain for all of us.

One day, Noah, my son who lives in Austin, Texas, showed up at my bedside and sat down in the chair for visitors. I had told him he didn't need to come, and it was true—I could have managed without him. He and his wife were both teaching full-time, and they had a first grader and a new baby at home to take care of. I had told him that other loved ones were checking in on me. My sisters were helping, and Sandy was going to come up from Los Angeles after I got out of rehab and stay with me at home to help out.

Noah came anyway. I was almost as happy to see him as I was on the day of his birth. How did he find his way into that chair by my bed, this man whose bed I had sat beside when he was a child? It was the first time I experienced this reversal. How strange and tender it was. He stayed for a few days, sleeping in my house and sitting with me in the rehab center during the day. He asked me how I was feeling, he listened, he showed me pictures of his children. While he was there, he gave me his undistracted attention, never seeming in a hurry. He managed things, too, like talking to the rehab doctor about changing my meds and arranging for a rented hospital bed to be delivered to my house before my discharge. I didn't want him to stay long, because I knew his family and his students needed him, but I was glad he came and deeply moved by his visit. I trusted that he came without reservations, and I received his help without guilt. A more positive way to say it is he came with love and I accepted his help with love. We weren't measuring anything.

I know that many old people don't have grown children who can or will help them. I'm lucky I do. Help can also come from friends and extended family, from people in your communities: from your neighborhood, schools, workplace, gym, church, temple, sangha. Important support is provided in a much more structural way in residential communities for seniors, both independent living and assisted living, and at the far end of the spectrum, memory care facilities and nursing homes. I was exploring the possibility of moving into a residential community myself until Francie and Bob agreed to move into my house with me, and now we have our own very small community of three.

Wherever you live, you will probably need help. Sometimes, help might not be offered the moment you need it, and you will have to ask for it. This is still the practice of accepting; you are accepting the fact that you need to reach out for help. Our culture values independence even at the expense of connection; it's considered shameful to need help. I now see that asking for and receiving help can be a kindness, because you are modeling for people who need help that it's okay to ask for it. So go ahead and ask: for a ride, for help with the computer, for checking the batteries in the smoke alarms. I don't yet need to ask for much, and when I need to ask for more, I hope not to be too stubborn about it. I've gotten really good at asking for help opening jars, and I'm lucky that I live with two skillful jar-openers. When I travel, I've been asking strong-looking strangers to lift my carry-on bag into the overhead bin. Last time, I asked a young woman and she graciously complied. "It feels good to be helped by a strong woman," I told her.

Asking for help can be a gift to those who help you, because most people, including old ones, are glad to have something to do that really helps. I know I am. For years I haven't had anyone who is dependent on me for help on a daily basis. As I have told you, my sons live far away with their wives and children. I'm single, and I retired some time ago from my nonprofit job in which I worked collaboratively with other people. For a number of years, it seemed that no one needed me on a daily basis except my cat, who depends on me to feed her, and on downhearted days I have wondered if this was enough to justify my usefulness on planet Earth.

Happily for me, since Francie and Bob moved in a couple of years ago, we help each other–cooking, washing dishes, reminding each other to take our vitamin pills. It's a joy to live with people I love. But even if they didn't live with me, I'd still be in reciprocal relationships with family and friends and communities in long-term ways. I rely on the connections between us, and so do they.

It can be hard to remember this reciprocity, but it's there, waiting for you to reach for it. I'm mindful of my friends who are single, who live alone, who have no one beyond themselves to make oatmeal for in the morning. I remember what that's like. Accepting that this is how it is right now, that you can cook your oatmeal exactly the way you like it, does not mean resigning yourself to loneliness and isolation. It means accepting that you need to take action in order to stay in relationship. All the more reason to ask for help and to find ways to give it.

Helping and being helped often turn out to be the same thing. I made soup for the new parents across the street, and when I delivered it, I got to hold the new baby. When I talk to a lonely friend on the phone, I feel much more connected myself.

All of us, whether living alone or with others, do indeed have someone who needs us on a daily basis, and that's our own dear selves. You can enjoy a friendly dialogue with the person you cook for ("How do you like your egg cooked, Sue?" "I don't want the yolk to be runny.") even if that person is yourself.

Practice dignity. You can be upright in your attitude even if your back is bent. Remember, you are Buddha.

A few decades ago, when I still thought of old age as a terrible disease that I hoped would never happen to me, a dharma brother at Berkeley Zen Center overturned my assumptions in a moving talk about his experience of getting old. I often reflect on it. He said that in his old age, it came naturally to him to put himself aside and not think about what he needed all the time. This was a great relief, he said, after decades of planning his life path; developing his career, his skills, his family life; and building an addition on his house. That was all behind him now, and he was at last free to stop thinking about himself. With no agenda of his own, he could fully delight in playing with his three-year-old grandson, whose happiness was as important to him as his own. They could build a tower together and knock it over, build it again and then knock it over again, laughing uproariously every time. Wow! In that moment in the zendo, I understood that getting old might make it easier to let go of self-clinging. Neither physical strength nor a good memory is required to pile some blocks on top of each other and knock them down again.

I've been talking about my four practices for old people, and now a fifth practice is jumping out at me.

Love (verb)

Even if you can't do much of anything else, you can love.

I think of my father going swimming with his two young sons from his late second marriage. He had three strikes against him: he was old, he was blind, and his legs were swollen and purple from cancer. I was middle-aged, visiting him in Cambridge from California, and one day I drove the three of them to the public swimming pool.

When I was a child, that same father had been sighted and athletic. Now, I watched him and the little boys come out of the men's locker room in their swimming trunks and walk across the slippery wet tile at the edge of the pool. *Please don't slip, please don't fall!* I prayed. My father–our father–turned and climbed slowly down the ladder into the pool. Determined to be a good dad, he called to the kids to jump in. He winced when his six-year-old crashed into his open arms, but my little brother didn't see it, and my father didn't make a noise. Then, joined by the nine-year-old, they played together, throwing a ball back and forth, my father finding the ball by its splash or its tap on his torso. I'm guessing that his pain was displaced by the joy of swimming with his bouncy boys. It was about a year before he died.

Finally, getting old is about practicing love. Loving is something an old person can do at least as well as a young one. Bad short-term memory can't keep me from loving. Not knowing how to get to the knitting store can't keep me from loving. What I really want to say is that whatever else I lose, I'll be okay as long as I can love.

Will I Ever Wake Up?

I'VE BEEN ON the Zen path for a good forty years now and I still haven't had a Great Awakening during zazen. I *have* had moments of great sleeping during zazen, however, and I'm somewhat comforted by the remark of the fabled Master Bush Wak, who said, "How can you awaken if you are not asleep?" Still, *when* will I awaken?

When I first came to Zen, I hoped I would get enlightened. I thought that if I sat hard enough (*Sit harder, Sue! Sit harder!*), a moment would come when I would be flooded with love and I would understand the meaning of life, particularly the meaning of *my* life. That didn't happen. I learned over the years not to grasp for enlightenment in zazen, but sometimes I would think, *Now that I'm not grasping for it, don't I deserve to get it?*

I have had moments of insight, yes, when a light bulb has suddenly switched on in my head, like in the comics, and I've seen that I'm connected to the entire universe. But it hasn't happened on the cushion. Do those moments count? Or is there something the matter with me that obstructs true awakening?

I worry about this, because I'm a lay Zen teacher, and doesn't that imply that I have experienced enlightenment? I was drawn to Zen partly because I love the literature–the sutras, the koans, the poetry–and this literature is full of references to awakenings.

Satori and *kensho* are Japanese words for the Zen enlightenment experience. English translations, necessarily imprecise, include "enlightenment," "realization," "illumination," and "awakening"—words for something that cannot be put into words.

Some say satori refers to a greater, longer-lasting awakening and kensho to a smaller awakening, though I can't help wondering how one awakening experience could be smaller than another one. Isn't immeasurability a signature characteristic of enlightenment?

The two largest schools of Japanese Zen are Rinzai and Soto. I'm fortunate that the kind of Zen I practice is Soto, because enlightenment is not emphasized in our school and, in fact, the subject is somewhat taboo. Nobody has ever put me on the spot by asking, "Have you had satori yet?"

In the Rinzai tradition, your teacher gives you a koan, which is a story or question that helps you go beyond the boundaries of your habitual thinking (for example, "Does a dog have Buddha nature?"), and you meditate on it until you have a breakthrough, an experience of kensho. As I understand it, you go to your teacher to have your kensho confirmed—she or he lets you know, "Yes, you got it"—and then you're given another koan. I have great respect for this tradition and for the Rinzai teachers and practitioners I know. Whether Rinzai or Soto, we're dharma sisters and brothers.

In our Soto family, we sometimes study koans informally, and we talk about them together. These old stories are full of sudden illuminations. And yet, in our school, it is said that everyone is already enlightened, whether we realize it or not. Shunryu Suzuki Roshi, whose lineage I'm a part of, famously said to his students, "You are all perfect, exactly as you are, *and* you could use a little improvement."

Dogen Zenji, the thirteenth-century founder of the Soto school, emphasized that practice and awakening are one continuous activity—a verb, not a noun. Everyday life and life as an enlightened buddha are the same life. You don't have to go somewhere special or do something special. "Here is the place. Here the way unfolds," Dogen says.

Over the years, these teachings have helped me relax about not having experienced a Great Awakening. But the question lurks in the shadows: Can I truly wake up? And how will I know if I do?

I'm in a study group of longtime Zen practitioners, and one of the books we've explored together is Keizan's *Transmission of Light*, an eleventh-century Chinese text. Thomas Cleary, the translator, says in his introduction, "This is a book of instruction in the art of satori–Zen enlightenment. . . . Satori is said to be the key to inner freedom and independence, the door to higher knowledge, realized by all enlightened people."

Uh-oh. The key to the door? Cleary's words brought back my insecurity, and the stories in the book, wonderful as they are, added to my worries, as each one tells of the sudden awakening of an ancient Zen master. So where's *my* satori?

I trust my dharma brothers and sisters with whom I've been practicing for years. I found the courage to break the taboo and blurted out this question to the group: "Have *you* experienced enlightenment?" Everyone seemed both relieved and shy to talk about it. I noticed that people blushed a lot. The mood was almost like a junior high pajama party where the talk was of sex, and as the subject of enlightenment was aired, it was normalized. We went around the room and everyone said modestly, "I am not enlightened." As we talked, we led each other to the shared understanding that there's no such thing as being in a permanent state of enlightenment. It's not a place you get to, where you can rest on your laurels from that day forward. We told each other stories, with verbs, not nouns, about talking with a teacher, being on solo retreat, falling off a bicycle. Everyone had had moments of waking up, moments of going beyond the separate self, some during zazen and some outside of the zendo, and they were just that–moments. When we included awakenings outside the zendo, I, too, had had my moments, as I will tell you.

Maybe satori wasn't such a big deal after all. I saw that I had turned "enlightenment" into a thing I didn't *have*, a thing that hadn't happened to me. But it's not an either-or matter. It's not a line you cross, becoming different from everyone else who hasn't crossed that line.

What about the people in the old Zen stories who had sudden awakenings? Are they different from me? Here are a couple of my favorites.

First, a story about a young woman in eighteenth-century Japan who became a prostitute in order to support her family. (That's pretty different, for starters.)

> Ohashi was terrified by lightning. One day, during a violent thunderstorm, she sat zazen on the veranda of the brothel in order to face her fear. A bolt of lightning struck the ground in front of her. She fainted, and when she awoke, she saw the world in an entirely new way. Hakuin certified her enlightenment.

What a brave young woman! I wonder if I could be that brave.

Here's another enlightenment experience from ninth-century China:

> Asan was a laywoman who studied Zen with Master Tetsumon and was unremitting in her devotion to practice.
>
> One day during her morning sitting, she heard the crow of the rooster and her mind suddenly opened. She spoke a verse in response:
>
> The fields, the mountains, the flowers, and my body too are the voice of the bird—what is left that can be said to hear?
>
> Master Tetsumon recognized her enlightenment.

Both of these women experienced enlightenment while sitting zazen. Both of them went to their teachers, who certified their enlightenment. (I admit it seems strange that enlightenment needs to be certified. Isn't the person who sees the light the exact person who *knows* she has seen the light?)

Now I'm getting worried again. I can't help wondering why I haven't had such an experience. Is it because I've tried too hard? It's supposed to just happen. You're not supposed to try to *make* it happen, are you? Or are you?

Well, I have had experiences of opening. I have had moments of realizing I was interconnected with all beings. So, with the idea that these actual experiences might be worth considering, I mention some of them:

- When I had laughing gas at the dentist, when I was about eight, I floated up to the ceiling, beyond all pain and fear, and looked down at the little girl in the dentist's chair who was having a cavity filled. I knew I had been that child eons before, and perhaps I would be her again. That would be fine. I could hear the whine of the drill, but I was completely free, up there next to the ceiling.
- When I first heard my newborn baby cry, I realized that everything in the universe was born at the same time.
- While hiking in a wilderness area of the Mojave Desert, I paused to mop my brow and looked up to see an endangered bighorn sheep standing stock-still on a rock ledge six feet above my head. For a silent instant, we looked directly into each other's eyes and recognized each other as one being.
- When I woke up in the recovery room after a colonoscopy, I found myself in a realm of bliss. I had just landed on a planet where everyone was the embodiment of kindness, and they were dancing around my bed attending to my every need—another blanket, a sip

of water—whatever I needed before I knew I needed it. They knew because there were no boundaries between us.

- When I stood in the garden at Tassajara Zen Mountain Center, waiting for the crack of mallet on wood from the temple to ricochet down the valley to my ears, I was poised to strike the echo han with a mallet, to call the monks to zazen. I watched the drops of water from the sprinkler catch the last sunlight and spread its glitter over the garden. The mallet in my raised hand was ready, free from time, for a second, and the second lasted forever.

At first glance, these moments do not particularly resemble the moments in the old koans. I don't know whether Hakuin (Ohashi's teacher) would certify a moment of enlightenment that was due to a colonoscopy. But wait—I think he would! Yes, he would! I'm remembering this story:

An old woman went to hear Master Hakuin give a lecture. He said, "Your mind is the Pure Land, and your body is Amida Buddha. When Amida Buddha appears, mountains, rivers, forests, and fields all radiate a great light. If you want to understand, look into your own heart."

The old woman pondered Hakuin's words day and night, waking and sleeping. One day, as she was washing a pot after breakfast, a great light flashed through her mind. She dropped the pot and ran to tell Hakuin. "Amida Buddha filled my whole body. Mountains, rivers, forests, and fields are all shining with light. How wonderful!" She danced for joy.

"What are you talking about?" Hakuin asked. "Does the light shine up your asshole?"

Small as she was, she gave him a big push, saying, "I can see you're not enlightened yet!" They both burst out laughing.

I appreciate their teasing affection. *Of course* the light shone up her asshole! Hadn't she just told him that Buddha filled her whole body and mind?

And how different was my moment of eye contact with the bighorn sheep from Asan's moment of feeling that her body was the same as the rooster's voice?

Come to think of it, plenty of the Great Awakenings in the old stories happen outside of zazen. In fact, most of them do. A person awakens while sweeping or drinking tea or tripping and falling to the ground. What if my aha!'s are just as valid as the awakenings in the koans?

The experiences I mention have changed my view of life. They have stayed with me and given me faith that "I" am not separate. I forget about them as I go about the business of the day, of course, but a kind of faith remains in my bones. And I can come back to the memories. When I think there's not enough time, I can remember the timeless garden at Tassajara. When I feel disconnected, I can think of the bighorn sheep.

It's as if you are living in a room that you think is the whole world. You don't even know that there are walls around you until suddenly a window opens, the blinds are drawn aside, and you see a vast mountain range beyond. When the blinds are closed again and you can no longer see out, you don't return to your former limited view, because now you know that the mountains are there. You know that you live among them.

The moments I have described are not typical of everyday life; they are exceptional moments. But you don't have to give birth or have a colonoscopy in order to glimpse the infinite. I remember Norman Fischer saying that enlightenment comes frequently, in little glimpses that you hardly notice before they quickly fade away. It can happen many times in an ordinary day. It's nothing more than knowing, for a moment, that you are *alive*. I appreciate this reminder. I don't need to wait for a peak experience; I need only to be fully present in the wide valley of my life.

For me, these little slippages into vastness are often connected to light, like walking through the dining room at the exact moment when the sun is backlighting the purple tulips in the middle of the table. Maybe this is why I love the practice of photography, because of the way the light gives itself away, illuminating whatever it meets with no distinctions. I had an enlightening moment yesterday, quite literally, when I paused in my early morning walk at the Berkeley Marina to sit on a bench and look at the bay, and the light of the sun landed on my jacket, magically turned itself into heat, and warmed me up. I remembered with astonishment that this warmth was coming to me from ninety-three million miles away.

Everyday interactions with others can also be openings for me, reminding me of our infinite subatomic connections. Someone passes me a napkin at the deli counter before I ask for it. Later the same day, I watch a very little girl sliding around on her stomach on a slippery marble bench in the post office while her mother waits in line. She sees me looking at her, sees my pleasure. "I'm swimming!" she declares.

Even if I don't have satori during zazen, I believe my practice makes me more open to waking up outside the zendo. That zazen time of exchanging my breath with the breath of the universe makes me porous. I continue to discover that I am not separate after all, not from the toddler on the bench, not from the nursing assistant in the recovery room.

Nothing's missing after all. I've seen the light! If I can see it, you can see it. The sunlight falls on everyone it meets, without picking and choosing. We can all be lit up.

Wake up, take a nap, wake up again. It's as easy as falling off a log.

I follow the path of Zen because it makes me more likely to appreciate being alive while I *am* alive. It helps me understand that my life is not separate from any life. On a family camping trip in the Sierra Nevada, my eight-year-old granddaughter and I lay next to each other on our backs in our sleeping bags, surrounded by lodgepole pines, and looked up at the night sky. "Isn't it amazing," she said, "the way the trees make a big circle in the sky and point up to the stars?" "Yes, it is amazing," I agreed.

Grandma's Diary Sutra

Dream of a gentle guru sort of old man coming for me. I said, "I'm not ready."

He said–as he went away–"Don't worry–I won't come for you before you are ready."

–SYLVIA SHAW JUDSON'S DIARY, JUNE 5, 1977

THE OLD GURU in Grandma's dream was right. She was ready to die when the time came, as I will tell you, and I want to be ready for my death, too.

Decades before my grandmother had this dream, she used to take me for picnics of brown-sugar-and-butter sandwiches in the meadow behind her house, and she would read fairy tales aloud to me. The night she died, in that same house, I was asleep in the bedroom across the hall. She was eighty-one, and I was thirty-five.

Another forty years went by before the diary she had kept for the last few years of her life came into my hands. As I read and transcribed her words and looked at her drawings, it was as if her hands reached right out of the book and pulled me back into her life and into the time of her dying.

I transcribed Grandma's diary in order to honor her remarkable life and to share with my siblings her thoughts about living and dying. A deeper reason for this undertaking revealed itself as I typed. I wanted Grandma to show me that it's all right to die.

I devoted some time to this transcribing project. For a couple of months in 2015, in my house in Berkeley, I started each day with Grandma, visiting with her for half an hour or so, studying her handwriting, turning several pages of her blue-ink days into a few more paragraphs of Times New Roman, being faithful to her idiosyncratic spelling and punctuation. As I typed, the gentle meter of Grandma's life wove itself into mine, giving a sense of rhythm to my more chaotic days.

April 2, '78
A warm sunny Sunday morning. The little begonia I talk to–the way the Findhorn garden book says you should–is blooming its head off by the window. Three scilla showing blue outside & daffodils in pot buds. St. Matthews Passion on my radio–Sidney brought me waffles for breakfast–no hurry to get up–meeting [Quaker Meeting] not for another couple of hours

Grandma was my mother's mother; she was a Quaker and a serious and successful sculptor. My three siblings and I spent much of our childhood with her and our grandfather at the old family home, called Ragdale, outside Chicago. I was the oldest child, born at the end of 1942, and in my first few years of life I stayed often with Grandma and Grandpa because of the upheavals of the war.

The house was designed by Grandma's architect father and built the same year she was born, 1897. Behind the house, to the west, was a "bowling green," though no one ever bowled there as far as I know. Beyond that a meadow, and still farther west, past a split-rail fence that my great-grandfather had built, uncultivated prairie. All the porches—upstairs for sleeping, downstairs for dining or hammocks—were on the back side of the house, for the view west. It was a house built for the evening, for summer evenings most of all, when the low sun charged the porches and the rooms inside with gold. That summer evening light, I believe, pervaded my growing brain as well.

When Grandma was in her sixties and I had just started college, my grandfather died of a heart attack. Two years later, she married Sidney Haskins, a British-born Quaker with an old-world elegance. They were both members of the Lake Forest Friends Meeting, and Sidney had been widowed at the same time as Grandma. For the sake of simplicity and community, they moved from Lake Forest to Kendal, a Quaker retirement community in the country near Philadelphia, where they lived for the last five years of Grandma's life.

When Grandma and Sidney moved to Kendal, my mother, recently divorced and in her fifties, moved from Cambridge to Lake Forest and took up the project of turning Ragdale into a foundation where writers and artists could come for creative residencies. The ending of my mother's thirty-five-year marriage was a painful time for her. With Grandma's blessing, Mom threw herself into the restorative and generous work of turning her vision of an artists' retreat into a reality. In those early and informal years of the foundation, when she was the director, cook, and housekeeper, and even learned to drive the tractor to mow the meadow, she closed Ragdale to residencies for writers and artists for the last weeks of summer so that Grandma and Sidney could spend time there. Grandma wrote,

> *Summer at Ragdale drawing to a close.*
> *swinging in the hammock to make a breeze.*
> *with a glass of iced tea & E. B. White's letters and almost no clothes*
> *A chickadee swinging on the tall seeds of a prairie dock – so slim and pretty.*
> *Dismantled show in Highland Park library. Sold five pieces.*

—

The typing goes slowly, which I don't mind, because I'm in no hurry to finish this job. I have to stop often to study Grandma's sometimes illegible handwriting, trying out different interpretations of the hard-to-read places, like cracking a code, until all at once I see what it says (or not). Transcribing is different from reading. I notice the blue ink grow faint and then suddenly darken, and I know she must have refilled her fountain pen. It was her hand that moved across this very paper. My typed words lack the physical life of her blue-ink writing, but her thoughts still breathe, even on my laptop screen.

> *The experience of depth*
> *Here–looking out my window, I have a turning*
> *The tree–the clouds–the stars.*
> *The layers on layers of branches of the maple tree. Almost a mystical experience.*

I can understand how painters get obsessed by depth—making collages and glass paintings.
And sculptors showing the insides of things coming thru.
I am amazed by the veins in my hands and wrists.

———

Toward the end, there were days when she was in pain and her handwriting became hard to decipher, tiny and cramped and wandering on the page. *"Everyone must be seasoned with fire."* But mostly her days were peaceful—she writes often of the view from her bed. *"The big leaves from my dogwood sailing down—'La belle aujourd'hui'"*

The book in which Grandma wrote contains many layers of time. It's a leatherbound diary with my grandfather's name, Clay Judson, stamped in gold on the cover and a blank page for each day of the year 1955. But my grandfather never wrote in it. Not one to waste things, Grandma used this diary many years later for sporadic entries from 1976 to 1978, when she was seventy-nine, eighty, and eighty-one.

On the front page, where it says "1955 YEAR BOOK," Grandma crossed out 1955 and wrote "76–77–78." On the page for January 1, 1955, she wrote,

Kendal
October 1976
I will be eighty years old in June
Conversations with myself.
And things I would like to remember.

Some drawings of the trees outside her window follow on the next few pages. Her entries have no regard at all for the dates printed at the top of the page. Under the printed heading "Friday, January 7, 1955" comes her first dated entry.

Oct. 30–76
The sun rose deep apricot color with a streak of turquoise
The warm affectionate closeness of Sidney–so strong and firm.

—

In my years of Zen practice, I've grown to love the teachings that have come down to us from long ago, like the ungraspable *Heart Sutra*, most essential of all our Zen texts, a mysterious incantation I was immediately drawn to and comforted by: "There is no attainment, with nothing to attain." These texts have made long journeys, through many centuries, from one language to another, from one alphabet to another, across miles of ocean, to get to me and my fellow Zen folks.

Grandma's diary is an old sutra, too. After she died, my mother kept it. A few decades later, my mother died, and the diary moved to Philadelphia to sit in a box in my sister Francie's basement. After another ten years, Francie went on a big clearing-out binge, and she mailed me the journal in a bubble-wrap book mailer with a sticky note saying, "I thought you'd like to see this."

I hadn't known this book existed. When I opened the crumbling leather volume, I saw Grandma's heart laid open on the pages–her thoughts about death and art, her drawings of leaves.

Lucky me with so many to love.
Friends & family & Sidney to love
Still find comfort in beautiful things and flowers

—

I loved my grandmother. She let me play with her modeling clay while she worked in her studio, she patiently watched the plays my siblings and cousins and I performed using the tattered-but-magical costumes from the giant trunk in the Ragdale attic. She showed me that sacred and beautiful things were everywhere: a "sculpturesque" chipmunk seeming to pose on the stone wall, the shimmering of cottonwood leaves in the breeze, the way my little sister tilted her head when she was reading.

After Grandma died, I used to consult her about my life. Should I take a particular teaching job? Should I work at becoming a writer? She never answered me in so many words, but sometimes, looking at myself through her eyes, I could imagine what she might say.

Now Grandma's voice comes to me in a book with my grandfather's name on it, thanks to my mother's careful keeping, my sister's thoughtful caring. Grandma's refusal to heed the proper dates collapsed chronology, revealing time's plasticity. Sculptor that she was, she shaped time, so that her diary came like a letter to me, a letter that arrived many decades after it was mailed, without postage or mailing address.

Strangely, I happened in those days to be purposefully studying death, as I was preparing a series of talks for my Zen sangha on Buddhist views of mortality. I was a little afraid to read the diary, because of how sad it might make me feel. I retreated to my bedroom, closed the door, and spent a day and a half with the diary, time-traveling, reading both eagerly and slowly. It didn't make me sad after all, because it brought Grandma back to me. Yes, it's about death, and about life, too. The person who wrote this diary was definitely alive while she wrote it, and she noticed that she was alive.

We are still alive, too—I as I write this and you who are reading it. In every human culture, the living have an ongoing relationship with those who have died, in one way or another. The living and the dead talk to each other often, though sometimes it's hard for us to hear each other. In her diary, I could hear Grandma clearly.

There is always this question about a diary: Who is the writer addressing? Though her opening epigraph says "Conversations with myself and things I would like to remember," Grandma had an artist's

March from my sofa
ficus plant — like those we had at Astor St.

sense of being in communication with unseen others, and this feeling must have extended to her diary, even if unconsciously.

In any case, her words beckoned me close. My name is mentioned from time to time, as are the names of other family members. "Susan wrote and asked if I knew a good children's prayer for Noah & Sandy" [my children]. Or "I'm reading 'Zen Mind Beginners Mind' by [Shunryu] Suzuki, given me by Susie for Christmas." It makes me feel good to know I was in her thoughts.

I am moved, too, by subjects of broader interest. She speaks often about death, and she speaks about life with relish, not separate from death.

A sparrow hawk–beautiful–smallish–black & white head–red back & tail–killed a sparrow on our terrace & flew away with it in his claws–Extraordinary

———

I am touched by entries about her love of everyday life, her ability to be present. Every morning as part of my Zen practice, I say, "I vow to be grateful for this precious human birth." It's a worthy thought, but vague compared to Grandma's expressions of gratitude.

I left the window open a crack to hear the sound of the rain. Later the sun came and went sending racing cloud shadows across the green field–The clouds were in layers of different shades–travelling in different directions–the yellow leaves were blowing. Something to remember!

And birds:

Lovely snow–hungry birds–Sidney swept the bench & spread seed–much appreciated.

Sidney is a loving and beloved presence throughout; he not only feeds the birds but often brings Grandma breakfast in bed. One day she reports,

> *French toast and good music–2nd act of Madame Butterfly–*
> *for breakfast–also grapefruit. (I must remember "This too*
> *will pass")*

On another day she writes,

> *Sidney bringing my breakfast and his–waffles because it is*
> *Sunday*

and in different ink, which makes me think she added it later,

> *I prefer French toast.*

I like to see this edge, playful more than complaining. Her love was not sugary, and she even took a mischievous pleasure in speaking of things and people she found annoying.

> *After Meeting we often invite Dorothea Wood aged 87 to eat*
> *with us. She is a flavorsome old gal–but I wish she wouldn't*
> *put her tea bag in her water glass.*

———

Even as a child, I felt safe with Grandma, because I knew where I stood. If she thought I needed a haircut (and she usually did), she said so, though never meanly, and a moment later I might catch her staring at me with undisguised affection. I often saw her looking at my siblings this way, too. Even as she gazed at us so tenderly, she may have been turning us into sculptures in her mind.

She paid loving attention to the details of life.

Putting on clean underwear after a shower is nice. Having to be careful with every step for fear your knee will go out is not nice.

And made deep explorations into the meaning of life.

TV program on Rubinstein–
90 years old–He played the piano 3 times and was inter-viewed–almost blind. Wonderful face like a Buddist monk. Said he was never afraid & was free. Said he didn't believe in life after death but then he might be happily surprised. Said it was only–when he was 20–& after he tried to commit suicide– that he truly lived–Interesting.

———

Is she really dead? How could she be dead when I am learning only today, in my seventies, that she read many of the same books I read and loved the same poems, without me knowing it, like Theodore Roethke's "I learn by going / where I have to go." We overlapped, here on this side of the River Jordan, for thirty-five years. We belong to each other.

In April of 1978, the year she died, Grandma and Sidney went on a cruise from San Francisco down the coast to Mexico. She enjoyed the trip, but when they got home to Kendal, she collapsed with a bad back. She worked with a physical therapist and on May 22 reported,

My back is <u>much</u> better–O joy!

That's the third of the three sentences she wrote that day. I am struck by the juxtapositions. Here are the first two sentences:

I reread this journal and found a lot of boring repetition about
my breakfast and Sidney & nature especially.
I have suddenly thought that God immanent & God transcen-
dent are the same thing–that the Holy Spirit is just one encom-
passing reality–a good thought which does away with conflict.
(See Rilke, Duino Elegies*)*

She might have written the first sentence for possible future readers as well as herself, not wanting us to think her superficial. Or perhaps Sidney had recently annoyed her in some small way and she was in a crotchety mood. In the second sentence she turned her attention to more serious matters than breakfast, partly to reassure herself (and her readers?) that she cared about these spiritual concerns and partly because she really did care. A number of times in her diary she referred to the question of whether God is here right now within us and all around us or whether God is managing everything from heaven, and on this day she apparently came to some peace with it.

Her back was better, but a couple of weeks later, on June 6, at home at Kendal, she got up in the night to use the bathroom, fell, and broke her hip. I think this was the beginning of the end, as is often the case when an old person falls, although it was not apparent at the time. Grandma had to have surgery, and while recovering in the hospital, she contracted pneumonia. Ten days later, she was sufficiently recovered from both the surgery and the pneumonia to go home. She wrote about the surgery:

I remember only two pricks and then having lovely halluci-
nations about whatever wheeled vehicle I was on starting off
slowly and then gaining speed and turning and going up or
down in an elevator and once thru a tunnel. I just relaxed and
let it go. This persisted for some days every time I shut my eyes.

A few days later she recalled:

> *I went into the hospital sort of sick and then had pneumo-*
> *nia. It would have been so simple if this [pneumonia] could*
> *have ended a rich and mostly happy life. . . . The operation*
> *couldn't have been final–but if the pneumonia had been left*
> *alone–no antibio, no oxygen–it might have. Oh well–maybe*
> *the indignities of old age are part of the human lot?*

I visited Grandma at Kendal when she came home from the hospital, and I remember vividly a conversation we had. She told me that during the surgery she'd had the experience of dying; she was on a cart, being wheeled through a dark tunnel; all was peaceful and beautiful, and she wasn't afraid. She said she wasn't allowed to keep going into death. She had to come back into her life, and one of the reasons she had to come back was to tell *me* not to be afraid of death. Naturally, that conversation made a great impression on me; it did, and still does, make me feel less afraid of death. I was moved to find, some forty years later, the following entry in the diary:

> *Susan coming today. Joy! What can I give her to remember?*
> *How the dark tunnel predicted the experience of dying & how*
> *relaxed and interested I was & disappointed when we backed*
> *out. In no way scared.*

———

Grandma had a collection of sleeping pills she'd been saving to end her life if she felt the need to do so. She had told us about this: her husband, my mother, me and my siblings.

She wrote,

> *Talked with Janet, the psychiatric social worker who used to*
> *be at Kendal. I wanted to be certain that if a final last resort*

was ever needed that I wouldn't botch it. She said my pills did not deteriorate but that one would need an accomplice to be sure one was not disturbed. Refused to say if fifty was enough but I'm sure it is. Said they reacted differently on different people–and she didn't believe in it–thought it gave you a harder time in the afterlife. I believe the motive would determine that.

She told Sidney she was ready to die because she felt her affairs were "wound up."

Sidney said–"O my dear–that isn't all there is to life" and when we were sitting quietly holding hands–he said–"This gives me such a feeling of completeness" So maybe there is more– He says we have to take what comes (ugh) that maybe I'll be pushing him [in a wheelchair]! I wouldn't mind that.

———

Grandma continued to work with a physical therapist on recovering her strength after the hip surgery. Progress was slow, but she felt well enough to make her annual summer trip to Ragdale, which she very much wanted to do. She and Sidney were welcomed to Ragdale by my mother on August 6, and there she spent what turned out to be the last few weeks of her life. Francie arrived in the middle of August and stayed to help our mother look after her. Grandma was much frailer than she had ever been, and death was much more on her mind. Sometimes she joked about it. "If I die, I'll make room for somebody else to get into Kendal off the waiting list." One day she commented that someone she knew, a biochemist, had advised her that a good way to take the pills and keep them down was with a glass of orange juice.

I knew how the story ended, but even so, strangely, as my fingers tapped their way toward the end of Grandma's diary, I felt mounting suspense. Was she going to leave us? I knew the answer from my own direct experience, but the story of her last Ragdale summer written from her own point of view was new to me. She was telling me what happened, and I was listening.

Typing out the final passages, I thought about the practice of hand-copying the *Heart Sutra*, that foundational Buddhist text. This copying is a sacred and meditative tradition. Transcribing Grandma's diary, her sutra, has also been a sacred practice.

I cried as I typed the last few entries:

Aug. 15
One whole week of glorious summer days. . . . I am being spoiled but not pleased with my progress. Wear the brace half days. Do the bed walking as much as I can endure—which isn't very much & is agony.

   16
Pain very bad

And the last entry, three days before she died:

28
Lake Forest Hospital for bone tests scanner–& biopsy
Fancy new machine–trying
Precious time at Ragdale passing. Theo came
Still center–Inward Light–Love compassion joy & peace

Grandma kept her sleeping pills in a little pouch. She took them with her to the hospital, but they said she couldn't bring her own medications, so she gave the pouch to my mother for safekeeping. She had the "trying" bone scans mentioned above, and they wanted to keep her in the hospital longer and do a biopsy, to find out what was wrong with her. "I don't care what's wrong with me," Grandma said, "I want to go home!"

So, on August 27, my mother brought her back to Ragdale, against the doctor's wishes, and when they got there my mother gave Grandma back her pills, at her request. Francie and Mom were worried, but they had already promised not to stop her from taking the pills if that's what she wanted to do. Grandma wasn't saying; she might not have known herself until the last minute. She and Sidney had plane tickets to go back to Kendal on September 1. Francie telephoned me in California to say she thought I should come if I wanted to be sure to see Grandma before she died, and I flew with my children to Ragdale on August 31.

When we arrived, Grandma was lying on the living room sofa in the late afternoon, looking out at the view across the prairie, the sunlight touching her. Her stomach hurt a lot, but she wanted to stay downstairs until she saw the sun set. Sandy, who was seven, gave her a foot rub–he was good at massages, and he used to charge five cents for a shoulder rub or a foot rub, but this one was free. He was wearing a red T-shirt from the kids' gymnastic program at the YMCA. It said "PeeWee Club." Grandma told him, "I should be in that club; I peewee all the time!"

Later, after some of us–not Grandma–ate sandwiches for supper in the kitchen, we helped her up to her bed in the Blue Room, named for the blue flowers on the wallpaper. It was the room that had been her bedroom as a child. My kids came in and said good night to her, and I put them to bed. Then Mom and Francie and I sat with her while Sidney packed her suitcase, under her direction. Sidney had ordered an ambulance limo to pick them up the next morning and take them to the airport, and Grandma was going through the motions of getting ready for the trip. Sidney brought items out of the closet on their hangers and showed them to her. "No, leave that coat here. Yes, that dress goes to Kendal." We were all pretty sure the journey she was about to make did not require packing, but we kept on pretending that she and Sidney would be off to Philadelphia in the morning.

How strange it seems now that we didn't speak directly about what we all knew was happening. Maybe we felt we couldn't acknowledge it until the deed was really done, or we'd have to stop her. In Grandma's day, there was no medically sanctioned provision for ending one's life by taking medication; she was acting under the radar. We followed an improvised ritual, not rocking the boat, honoring Grandma's intentions and the promises of noninterference that she had extracted long before.

Our family culture was polite. This was, admittedly, an extreme form of politeness, and if you were watching the scene in a movie, you might even think it was funny. *What's with these people? They know the old woman–their wife, mother, grandmother, great-grandmother–is about to end her life and they're talking about which sweater she should take on the plane!*

The packing job was done, and Sidney snapped the latch of the suitcase shut.

Grandma asked Francie to bring her a glass of orange juice. She asked us to leave her alone. It was time to say good night, and *good night*, not *goodbye*, was the word I said when I leaned down to kiss her. I felt numb and slow, as if I were walking on the ocean floor in a heavy diving suit. We took our leave–Francie and Mom and Sidney and me. We went out and shut the door behind us.

Across the hall from Grandma's room, I tried to go to sleep. From down the hall I heard sobbing. I got up and followed the sound to Sidney's room and walked through the open door into darkness. I made out the figure of Sidney, standing in the middle of the room, just standing there, hands hanging at his sides, weeping loudly. It was the more heartbreaking because he was such a proper British gentleman and this seemed so out of character. But he loved my grandmother and was devoted to her care. No more bringing her breakfast in bed.

I said his name and hugged him. We stood together like that for a while and he cried on my shoulder.

Early in the morning Francie went into Grandma's room. "It worked," she told me when she came out. "She's dead." I went into the Blue Room and stared at Grandma's body, and by the shape of the mound under the blanket I saw that she was curled up like a child on her side. Her face and one hand emerged from the blanket, white against the white pillow.

This was the first dead body I had ever seen, and I was shocked at how obviously dead it was. I say "it" because I could see instantly that Grandma wasn't there. I guess I hadn't anticipated that. Perhaps I expected that a person who had just died, apart from staying still, would look exactly the way they had looked when they were alive. I saw that her body was unoccupied. It wasn't only the waxy whiteness of the skin but also the way the skin hung on her face and how her face looked thinner, smaller. There was no feeling left in it. Not one of the hundreds of muscles in the face was working any more. I wonder if this is what people mean when they say someone looks peaceful after death. I think a person looks peaceful when they *feel* peaceful, not when their face has no expression at all.

On Grandma's bedside table was a folded piece of paper that said "For Family" on the outside. Inside the fold was a note that appeared, by the extreme neatness of the handwriting, to have been prepared some time before, in case the occasion should arise.

> *Darlings—Before going off to sleep—I want to say what you know of course—that I love you—and am grateful for your love of me and know that you would have continued to cherish me—but to choose not to go on suffering seems to me the simplest of human rights. Thanks for everything and bless you—*

There was also a note on a small scrap of paper, which she must have written as she was dying. The handwriting is barely legible and turns into illegible squiggles before it stops entirely.

I hope that happily accepting and going to meet what is inevi-
table [illegible] when the moment seems right and one still has
the ability can make decision [illegible] my brain my hands
my eyes my ears my memory are all diminishing fast

The *Heart Sutra*! I thought of it and was startled by the resonance.
When I'm afraid, like on a bumpy flight, or when I'm lying sleepless
in the middle of the night, I say the *Heart Sutra* to myself, including
the strangest line of all: "no eyes, no ears, no nose, no tongue, no body,
no mind . . ."

Grandma had put a sign on top of the blanket, at the foot of her bed.
It was part of her death kit–she had kept it with her pills in a little woven
bag for this very occasion. It was the kind of sign you hang on the door-
knob of your hotel room, and she had gotten this one in Nairobi. On one
side it said, "Do Not Disturb." On the other side, the side that she had put
face up, it said the same in Swahili. Her last joke.

I left the house and hurled myself down the lane, running as fast
as I could through the dewy grass to Grandma's sculpture studio. A
carved wooden angel from the nineteenth century, with wild hair and
a craggy face, probably ten feet tall, hung high on the outside wall of
the studio. My great-grandfather had somehow gotten this angel in
France and had shipped him back home, and the angel had looked
down from the studio wall as far back as I can remember. I stopped,
panting and sweating, beneath him. "Please take care of Grandma," I
cried. "If you see her."

When I got back to the house the others were awake. I asked my
children if they wanted to see Grandma's body. Noah, who was ten,
said no, and Sandy, who was seven, said yes. He came in and stared
for a minute at her face. The feet he had massaged the day before
were under the blanket. Years later he told me it was scary, and he
wished he hadn't gone in. It was my mistake. He probably thought

that because I asked him, he was supposed to say yes. Noah, a little older, was able to say no. Now I realize that if we had had a cultural frame for seeing Grandma's body, like a Catholic wake, or a Buddhist vigil with the body, it might have been less frightening, but we had no ritual for sharing grief in that moment.

My mother didn't want to go into the Blue Room either. She made some phone calls, then went downstairs and sat on the living room sofa, with the view of the prairie, to wait for the people who were going to pick up the body for medical research. Francie went with her to keep her company. I don't remember what I did next, but I must have made breakfast for Noah and Sandy. I do remember, a little later, watching out the front window as two men loaded the covered body into a van and drove away. I couldn't help thinking about how medical students were going to cut up her body in order to learn how a human being works. That's what Grandma wanted.

Later that day we found yet another tiny note in the drawer of the bedside table, in the very shaky handwriting of the last few days:

> *it should be given out that I had a stroke (which I think I have*
> *so it would not be a lie) & I should hate to make it any easier*
> *for a young person or anyone with any deprision or anything*
> *that might be temporary to follow suit.*
> *I have had a long & satisfying life & don't want to be greedy.*
> *There is even a chance of seeing those I have loved in the past*

———

I respect, even admire, my grandmother's decision. I think she was brave. She had had eighty-one full and creative years, she was in pain, and she didn't want to be dependent on others. But my respect for her decision didn't keep me from being torn up by her absence. Isn't it a mystery that absence can hurt?

Your life doesn't belong to you alone. Your life belongs to everyone who loves you. Grandma took her life, as the saying goes; indeed, she "took her life" away from all of us, and we didn't try to stop her. She was on the stubborn side, and we knew we had to let her go. Besides, it's not as if we had a choice. The choice was hers. Even if your life doesn't belong to you alone, maybe your death does. Grandma chose her end time and took off, dropping her heartbeat into some hidden chasm as she departed. But the Grandma who lives inside me doesn't need a beating heart–she can share mine. I animate her with my thoughts and with these words I'm writing. You could say I'm making her up, but she's making me up, too.

Quite naturally, I think about death more as I get older. I'm further from Grandma's death in time and yet her death comes closer to me as I get closer to my own.

Grandma had tucked this note into her diary:

Voluntary death
Pros
Sparing your family and friends as well as yourself and attendants
(after you can no longer be brave & cheerful & contribute)
Not spoiling the memory of you by getting to be like Ellen S. or Bertha DuBois or Amy
Releasing your place to someone younger and money for creative use. [a reference to Kendal, her retirement community]
Cons
Making your family feel guilty or hurting them
Upsetting the community [Kendal, again]
Would rather not do anything that had to be secret
Better to be an example of cheerfulness & courage (if possible) and sharing the common fate

It would have been better, kinder, for Grandma and for the rest of us if she had had medical permission to do what she did. She could have done it openly. Still, she demonstrated that a person doesn't need a physician's assistance to end her life with dignity. She knew we would be sad, but wouldn't we have been just as sad if she died later, after months or years of pain?

Most religions, including Buddhism, have some stricture against suicide. I've taken the Buddhist precepts, the first of which is the vow "not to kill, but to nurture life." A Zen friend who volunteers with hospice patients told me, "I'm not afraid to die. I won't take pills, but I won't accept any extreme treatment either. I'll let nature take me." Another Buddhist friend with a different point of view worked hard for the Death with Dignity Act in California, which was successfully passed in 2016. It allows "physician-assisted dying," meaning you can get a doctor's prescription for a lethal dose of sleeping pills if you are terminally ill and expected to die within six months.

I'm glad it passed, but even if I qualified, I don't know whether I would exercise this option. I might hesitate too long, putting off making a decision from day to day. I might take the first precept too literally to let myself do it. I might not want to, because of curiosity about what still might happen in my life, or because consciousness by its nature wants to hang on to consciousness as long as possible. I might want to stay alive a little longer, still hoping to get *really* enlightened before I go, like Tolstoy's Ivan Ilyich, who saw the light at the last minute. Or I might be too far gone into dementia to lift the glass and swallow the pills myself.

On the other hand, I might be in pain and ready to go. I just don't know. Not yet. Grandma has helped me trust that I'll know when I need to know. Like every other human being, I'll cross that bridge when I come to it whether I like it or not.

My engagement with Grandma's diary has made me less afraid of dying and happier to be alive. These two feelings are actually one feeling. Grandma was able to take her leave without fear because she had relished her life–Sidney's French toast and the birds at the feeder.

Nov. 21, 1976
How much happiness in just the one view out the window
from my bed–The stars are in different places if you wake in
the night–the clouds shift–the sun rises the birds begin to come
to the feeder. cardinals are always early.

Some of My Favorite Practices for Contemplating Death

Seven wise sisters planned a spring journey. One of them said, "Sisters, instead of going to a park to enjoy the spring flowers, let's go together to see the charnel grounds."

The others said, "That place is full of decaying corpses. What is such a place good for?"

The first woman replied, "Let's just go. Very good things are there."

When they arrived, one of them pointed to a corpse and said, "There is a person's body. Where has the person gone?"

"What?!" another said. "What did you say?" And all seven sisters were immediately enlightened.

−KOAN FROM *THE BOOK OF SERENITY*, SEVENTH-CENTURY CHINA

WHY DID WE come here if we're only going to leave again? What's next? Death is the big question mark in life. In Buddhism and Christianity, and probably in other religions, too, the deliberate contemplation of death is a traditional spiritual practice. It may seem counterintuitive, but I speak of death contemplations here not to be ghoulish but to raise your spirits. See if it works.

I'm curious about my own absence as it approaches me. Is it the same absence that preceded my birth, a goneness that envelops me at either end? Zen Buddhists sometimes ask, "What was your face before your parents were born?" That's a good question! But most of the time we don't wonder nearly as much about where we came from as where we're going. We think that what happens after we die is in the future, a gift we haven't opened yet, and we suppose that before-we-were-born is in the past: been there, done that. It's all used up. As if time goes in only one direction. But is the place we come from really in the past? How could it not be the same place as where we're going? When we die, maybe we just pick up where we left off when we were born.

I have an urgent wish to understand these matters. In my Zen practice and in my personal explorations, I have learned some ways to have a conversation with death. Strangely, I have found that when I deliberately consider my own death, I feel more alive. Here I share some of my favorite death contemplations, in the spirit of sharing favorite recipes. Some of them might be to your taste.

The Five Remembrances

Buddha urged his disciples to meditate upon the five remembrances. When I first heard them, I thought, *Wow! This is harsh!* But I shouldn't have been surprised; they are straightforward reminders of the teaching of impermanence. Here is Buddhist teacher Thich Nhat Hanh's translation.

- I am of the nature to grow old. There is no way to escape growing old.
- I am of the nature to have ill health. There is no way to escape ill health.
- I am of the nature to die. There is no way to escape death.
- All that is dear to me and everyone I love are of the nature to change. There is no way to escape being separated from them.

- My actions are my only true belongings. I cannot escape the consequences of my actions. My actions are the ground on which I stand.

The first three on this list—old age, sickness, and death—are the three
forms of suffering the young prince Shakyamuni saw when he first left
the protection of his father's palace before he became the Buddha, and
each of these remembrances helps us to savor the life we have now and
not to grasp for permanence. It is our clinging to youth, health, and life
that causes suffering. This is a difficult teaching, but familiar to me.
The fourth remembrance—that I will lose everything I love—was at first
unexpected and unbearable for me: *I'll be ripped away from everyone
I love, one way or another. My heart will be in tatters!* See how I make
it worse by fear and clinging? When I stay with it, when I say it gently
to myself, this remembrance helps me to love right now the people who
are dear to me and urges me not to hang on to them too tightly, because
that will only cause more pain on both sides. I wouldn't want to hear,
"Ouch, Grandma! You're squeezing me too tight!"

The other day, I was talking on FaceTime with my granddaughter
Sally in Virginia—three thousand long miles away. These days, because
of the pandemic, I can't hug her, even gently. Sometimes I think: *Face-
Time-ShmaceTime! My whole body aches to hug her.* On this call we
were playing a drawing game, and we propped up our phones so that
we could see each other. It was Sally's turn to draw something for me
to copy, and she was silent for a couple of minutes, concentrating. In
that interlude, I could hear the scratch of her pencil. I looked at the top
of her head as she bent over her paper, the shine coming off her curly
hair, shifting as she changed the tilt of her head in the light from the
window. I stopped clinging. I had all I wanted. That's the joy hiding in
the fourth remembrance.

The fifth remembrance—that my own actions are all I have—comes as
a gift, encouraging me because I have some agency. I'm not completely

helpless after all. My actions have consequences, which is another way of saying that my actions make a difference. The law of karma gives me a fresh chance in every moment to act out of love. The fifth remembrance tells me the good news that I'm not just the victim of blind fate; I have a say in what form my impermanent life takes.

When I learned about them, I took up the practice of saying the five remembrances to myself every morning for a month, and they stopped seeming harsh and became good medicine. The more I accept my impermanence, the more *here* and the more *now* I can *be*. And when I understand that I will lose everything, I see that I have nothing left to lose, so everything around me is a bonus. It's all borrowed from the great library of the universe and will have to be returned on the due date.

Considering our intractable impermanence, it's quite heroic how we keep on taking out the recycling, how we raise and educate children even though they are going to die—every single one of them—how we throw ourselves into making things that will someday burn or break or be forgotten. The whole time we know we're all going to end up dead anyway. But we're not dead yet; we're alive together, and it's a joint project—breathing.

Every once in a while, I renew my attention to the five remembrances so they don't get rusty. If you decide to try them out, I suggest you read them out loud to yourself first thing in the morning. You could even fortify yourself with a cup of coffee as you read. Give them at least a week.

Walking in Cemeteries

Cemeteries are gathering places for the dead. When you walk in a cemetery, even if you're going there to visit one particular grave, you can't help noticing that you're not the only one who has lost an ancestor. I like to walk in cemeteries that have beautiful plants and trees, and see the intermingling of life and death, the birds nesting in the trees above the gravestones.

When I was in elementary school in Cambridge, Massachusetts, the science teacher occasionally took us for bird walks in nearby Mount Auburn Cemetery, a nature preserve as well as a burial place. I was distracted from the birds by the graves, which fascinated me. I tried to read the writing on the gravestones as we were herded along, to see how long the people had lived, and it made me sad when there was a child underneath. I asked about a pink marble building the size of a small house among the graves. What was it for? Did someone live there? No, it was called a mausoleum, and somebody's body was in it, in a coffin. I wondered but didn't ask why they wanted to be in this empty building. It seemed better to be buried underground, where your dead body would have more privacy.

Later, at recess, one of the other kids taught us a chant:

The worms crawl in, the worms crawl out,
The worms play pinochle on your snout,
And one little worm that isn't so shy
Crawls in your left ear and out your right eye.

As I chanted, I pictured a body buried in the dirt, crawling with worms. The use of the second person in the chant packed a punch. "*Your* snout" meant the chant was telling me it would happen to me, too. That would be my body.

This was our third-grade version of the third remembrance: "I am of the nature to die. There is no way to escape death." When I was eight years old, that line would have been too abstract to touch me or too scary for me to hear, but the worm chant, because it was gross and funny—*What's pinochle, anyway?*—delivered its profound message.

On a visit back to Cambridge a couple of years ago, my friend Fanny took me for a walk in Mount Auburn Cemetery, many decades after the bird walks. It's the most beautiful cemetery I know. It was a June evening, and the whole park glowed in the late sun: trees, shrubs, curving pathways. We heard birds singing good night and frogs croaking. Life abounded among the graves. Fanny showed me the plot she had reserved for herself and said she could hardly wait to lie down and rest in this beautiful spot. Fanny alive and Fanny dead were both at home here, where the last of the season's lilacs were still in bloom.

Cemeteries can make you sad. While visiting a friend in Corvallis, Oregon, I went for a walk and came upon a small graveyard with big shade trees. One weathered granite stone read:

R.C. WHITNEY
Died
May 17, 1869. Aged
1 yr. 1 mo. & 1 dy

By cool Siloam's shady rill
The lily must decay.
The rose that blooms beneath the hill
Must shortly fade away.

Siloam, I learned later, was a pool near Jerusalem, where Jesus healed a blind man. That day in Corvallis, I could just make out the words under the pale-green lichen that now spotted the stone. Seeing the shortness of the life, I cried. I stood still, thinking of the baby who had lived a year, a month, and a day, and of her parents. Had they found a strange comfort in the terrible poetry of that time span? Had they said to each other, "We only had her with us for a year, a month, and a day"? I knew they had learned the lesson that everyone dies, because they had written that lesson on the gravestone: "The lily must decay. The rose . . . must . . . fade away."

It was a hot August afternoon, and I lingered in the shade of the old trees, listening to the sound of the Willamette River. I was old enough to be this baby's grandmother or even great-grandmother. And looking at time in the other direction, the baby was old enough to be my great-great-great-grandmother, if she had lived to bear children. In any case, I understood that we were members of the same family. I caught sight of how much suffering there is in our family, and I caught sight of how much love.

Making a Day of the Dead Altar

Every year around November 2, the Day of the Dead, I make an altar just inside the front door of our house, in the Mexican tradition, on which I place photos of loved ones who have died, along with flowers and candles and little skeletons and maybe some extra Halloween candy. I learned about this tradition when I went to Oaxaca, Mexico, with my sister Francie, to celebrate my sixtieth birthday. My birthday also happens to be November 2, so I have a personal connection with the Day of the Dead. They celebrate my birthday in a big way in Mexico, and that year, I went to the party. For several nights the cemeteries of Oaxaca were lit up with strings of holiday lights and the paths and gravestones were strewn with marigolds. Listening to the music of the strolling bands, we walked among groups of relatives gathered at the graves to eat and drink what their deceased loved ones liked best. It reminded me of the Thanksgiving holiday in the US, when the extended family comes together, only some of the people at this celebration were alive and some were dead. The mood was festive. And in the streets of the town, in every doorway and courtyard, were exuberant altars, covered with marigolds and photos, toys and candy. We saw how porous is the line between life and death in Mexican culture.

I encourage you to make a Day of the Dead altar in your home and leave it there for a week or so. Spread a bright cloth over a small table and put some candles on it—you can get convincing electric candles these days if you don't want live flames in the house. You can decorate the altar with photos and other mementoes of your loved ones, like your father's pocket watch or a box of the mints your mother liked. Or add autumn leaves and fruits and flowers. I try to get marigolds, because their bright orange color and distinctive smell remind me of Mexico. I put out skeletons I've collected over the years, including a skeleton at a typewriter who sits on my desk the rest of the year, reminding me to write while I'm still alive.

Last year I invited a few friends to come over on the evening of the Day of the Dead and to bring for the altar a photo of someone they loved who had died in the past year. I lit the candles on the altar; offered wine, tea, and pumpkin pie in the Oaxacan spirit of celebration; and we hung out together. Then by turn we told each other about the people in the photographs. We living people were celebrating our dead people, we were witnessing each other's love for the departed ones, and we were welcoming them back into the room as our guests. One friend cried as he spoke of the woman who had taught him to juggle. He's an old friend, but I had never seen him cry before. Our individual griefs blended into one grief so that none of us was alone, and the people who had already died, the ones we cried for, sat together on the altar, keeping each other company, so they weren't alone either. You could create a gathering like this, too.

I couldn't have such a gathering this year because of the COVID-19 pandemic, even though so many people were dying. But I made an altar and found comfort in it. I leaned a skeleton playing the fiddle against the photo frame in which my late friend Susan smiled out at me. I arranged the objects: the rusty-red chrysanthemums, the bar of dark chocolate with tangy chili (her favorite), the sugar skulls that I bring out every year, an orange persimmon, and a few tangerines. She would like–or she *does* like–all the brightness.

Reading Obituaries

I recommend the practice of reading the paid death notices in the local newspaper, whether in print or online. I'm not talking about the obituaries of well-known people, which I read out of historical interest. No, the point of this practice is to read about the lives of ordinary people, strangers to me. They have all died, and so will I. For me, the cumulative and unexpected effect of reading these notices is a sense of affection for my fellow humans, along with the realization that every life is extraordinary, no matter how ordinary it seems. Here is a collage of excerpts from the *San Francisco Chronicle.*

The odd details are touching: "*A 40-plus-year employee of PG&E, Patrick, with six children, several with crooked teeth and all attending Catholic schools, never hesitated to work overtime or help PG&E crews on stormy nights. . .*"

And funny: "*Devoted Daddo would do anything to get his grandkids to laugh, from releasing an earth-shattering burp in the carpool lane to cannon-balling into the pool with all his clothes on.*"

Outside of my usual frame of reference: "*Lou began his enduring love of the science of flight as a youth. Early on he identified all the planes in NY City's skies during the thirties and forties.*"

I read of simple pleasures: "*Deedee loved crime shows, sitting in the sun, and spending time with her loved ones.*"

Of a young death: "*Dennis died doing what he loved, riding his Harley on his favorite road on a beautiful day.*"

Of generosity: "*Following her retirement from Cowell Hospital, Dr. Chapman volunteered to work for one year as the only physician at Sherubtse College, in Kanglung, Bhutan . . .*"

Every kind of person dies. Including, let us remember, the people who can't afford a paid notice.

When I shared my practice of reading death notices with a friend in her eighties, she tried it, too, and she said it came as a great relief. As she approached the end of her life, she'd been feeling disappointed in herself–she hadn't accomplished as much as she'd hoped as an artist. She wondered what her life meant. What had she really given? (I happen to know she's given a great deal, and I know how easy it is for artists to think that their work hasn't made enough difference.) Reading the death notices moved her. "I saw that ordinary life was somehow beautiful. Everybody's life was meaningful. Everyone was completely who they were–and so am I," she said.

Me, too. These doctors and sunbathers, burping grandpas and motorcycle riders, remind me to be myself right now and to offer what I have to offer. I don't have time to turn myself into somebody else who can offer what somebody else offers. I'm a human being who's going to die, and I have the chance to be alive, as me, until I'm dead.

Try this practice in a deliberate way. Read two or three death notices every day, for a week, and see what happens.

Writing Death Poems

You can contemplate your death by writing a poem about it, and you don't have to be a poet to do it. The tradition comes to us from Japan, where, from the eighth century onward, it was customary for samurai warriors, Zen monks, and, yes, poets to write a final poem when they were close to death. (The following examples come from a wonderful book called *Japanese Death Poems*, compiled by Yoel Hoffmann.)

The death poems of Zen monks were often poignant reflections on the natural beauty of "the floating world," the world we inhabit while we live.

> This is the last day
> I shall see the mallards
> crying over Lake Iware.
> Then I shall disappear
> into the clouds.

It was considered a tour de force to write a poem at the very last minute. A fifteenth-century poet and warrior, Ota Dokan, was stabbed as he was bathing. He pronounced the following poem in the moments before he died:

> Had I not known
> that I was dead
> already
> I would have mourned
> my loss of life.

Zen death poems often bring a lightness to the subject of death, as if to say, "Let's not take ourselves too seriously."

> Should someone ask
> where Sokan went,
> just say,
> "He had some business
> in the other world."

And a wide perspective, as if the speaker has already moved beyond his own personal self.

Empty-handed I entered the world,
Barefoot I leave it.
My coming, my going–
Two simple happenings
That got entangled.

Some monks followed the tradition of writing a death poem every new year and tucking it into the sleeve of their robe to replace last year's poem, like updating their will. This way, if they should die on the road, they'd at least have a death poem handy that was no more than a year old.

In a discussion group on death that I was leading, we all wrote our own death poems and read them to each other. This was rewarding, even joyful. I recommend it. Writing one can help you lighten up, get beyond yourself, and accept your death. Try it by yourself or with friends.

A few suggestions: Keep your death poems short, as is the convention. Centuries ago in Japan, they were usually in the tanka form, with five lines of 5-7-5-7-7 syllables, in that order. You could follow this form, just for fun, or vary it by counting the words instead of the syllables. You could use the haiku form–three lines of 5-7-5 syllables. Or use no particular form at all. In any case, if you write death poems with friends and read them aloud to each other, I predict it will make you love each other more than ever. Here are a few that came out of our group exercise.

By a potter:

Come from clay:
A fine, strong, upright vessel,
Holding love, fear, gratitude,
Now returning to earth's body.
      –MARY LAW

A gardener's haiku:

> Let the weeds rejoice
> Over my remains, free from
> My grasping fingers.
> —SUSAN ASHLEY

And one from me:

> Once I was inside a star
> Now I'm here. I've come quite far!
>
> My name is Sue, but not for long.
> Soon I'll join the massive throng
>
> Of those who've given up their names—
> Like Mary, Friedel, Ned, and James.
>
> My bag of skin will let me out
> And I'll no longer think about
>
> The list of things I have to do.
> You'll be me and I'll be you.
>
> When I hand in my dinner pail
> My love will carry on full sail.

The Sorting Sisters

Let one not be submerged by the things of the world.
—THE *METTA SUTTA*

Y OU DON'T HAVE to sort alone.

We call ourselves "The Sorting Sisters." There are five of us, and we are helping each other to organize and downsize our possessions, giving each other moral support in a difficult task. We are all in our seventies, a time of life when subtraction is positive and addition is negative. As time goes by, the boxes in our closets, garages, attics, and basements get heavier with the weight of the past.

What do we do with the bundles of letters containing forgotten dramas? What do we do with the carousels of slides holding mind-altering sunsets we can no longer remember and no projector with which to see them? We need each other's encouragement.

We sorters have come up with an excellent method. Every third Saturday, for five hours in the afternoon, we meet the only way we can these days, on Zoom. We have been doing this since early in the pandemic, the spring of 2020, and Zoom is the perfect vehicle. We are each in our own home, where we have to be, of course, in order to sort, and at the same time we are together, as we have to be in order to support. Sort and support. That's what we do.

At the beginning of every meeting, each of us describes her project for the day. We might show each other on the screen a cluttered desk, an overflowing bookcase, or a stuffed file drawer. We sort for a couple of hours and come back to the Zoom room to report on our progress. We often have show-and-tell, sharing surprising discoveries we made. After a second sorting session, we have a final meeting to report on how the day went.

I engage in this sorting behavior to make it easier for those who will have to take care of my stuff, postmortem. I don't want to leave a mess behind me.

After I'm dead, I doubt I'll care if my children are complaining about boxes of unsorted photographs, archaeological potsherds that were on my mother's desk when she died, my extra office supplies, a set of demitasse cups I never use, and bundles of letters from old friends held together with brittle rubber bands that break when you touch them—I can feel my anxiety rising even as I list these things—but I do care now, ahead of time. You could call it precognitive caring.

The house I've lived in for forty-nine years, the house my children grew up in, the house I now share with Francie and Bob, my sister and brother-in-law, has ample storage space in the attic and the basement—a plus and a danger. The boxes of old letters aren't doing any harm while I'm alive and in residence. But I'm a person who tends not to complete a job until the last minute, and who knows when my last minute will be? Even if I do learn, down the road, that the last minute will come in a matter of days, I won't be rising from my deathbed to sort the ski equipment. I need to get down to business now for the sake of my children, and the Sorting Sisters spur me on.

I came across a helpful book called *The Gentle Art of Swedish Death Cleaning* by Margareta Magnusson. When I first heard of it, I thought the title was a joke, but no, it turns out that the phrase *death-cleaning* is a standard idiom in Swedish. In Sweden, cleaning your home in preparation for your death is seen as a normal and natural task. Magnusson reminds us that death-cleaning is an act of basic courtesy to those who will have to pick up after us.

A second great benefit of sorting is the creation of a simpler, less cluttered environment to bask in now while you are still breathing. It's nice to have empty surfaces here and there where you can put down the mail when you first bring it in. (But don't leave it there!) It's great to have more room in a room. The sunshine looks better when it comes into a room where it has flat places to land on. Your mind can be less cluttered, too, if you don't keep seeing the broken lamp in the corner waiting for you to do something about it.

A third reason for sorting: Even if you don't get rid of anything, organizing what you have can improve your quality of life. It's so pleasant to be able to find the stapler when you need it.

My Zen practice has encouraged me in all of this. The Zen aesthetic is simple and spare—one flower in a vase on an empty table. Live a simple life. Don't take more than you need. Chop wood and carry water. Many of my Zen friends are well sorted, especially those who are in residential practice and have only one small room to call their own, with few possessions beyond the traditional monk's robe and bowl. When I lived at Tassajara Zen Mountain Center for three months, I loved having only the bare minimum, though I can't take much credit for this renunciation. For one thing, I had a stash of constantly replenished chocolate bars sent to me by friends in the outside world; and for another, I was only temporarily playing at the simple life and would soon return to my comfortable home with Francie and Bob. I'd rather live with them than with a robe and a bowl, but I'm grateful for having tasted plain living. I'm motivated to take small steps in that direction, with the help of the Sorting Sisters.

Zen teachings are always talking about emptiness, and I've tried to do my sorting with a spirit of emptiness. Not needing extras. Making do with what I have as long as it works. Accepting that every single thing is "empty of self-nature" and has no permanent existence in a particular form. A mug that was given to me by a grandchild sits on my desk.

The words on the mug say "I'm a Grandma. What's your superpower?" I love this mug, but in a way, the mug is already broken. If I drop it on the floor and it shatters, I'll remind myself that it's only revealing the impermanence that was already there. I'll say, "Hey, Sue, everything is already broken!" But I might cry a little bit, too.

When my sister Nora moved from Santa Fe to Berkeley about twenty-five years ago, she and her daughters arrived at their unfurnished rental house a few weeks before the moving van. In the interim, Nora and the kids slept on borrowed mattresses on the floor and scrounged a few necessities from friends and thrift stores. I joined them for some excellent picnics, seated on folding chairs around a slab of plywood on milk crates. Our voices echoed mysteriously in the empty house. What had at first seemed like a huge inconvenience became a happy adventure, and by the time the moving van arrived, Nora was dreading the *having* of things–the tangle of unpacking, arranging, repairing, rearranging. Of course she got used to belongings again, and reassembled them to make a comfy home for herself and her kids, but for a brief respite she experienced the unadvertised pleasure of simple living, and she said it loosened her grip on things.

Even though I see the great benefits of sorting, the obstacles loom as large as a nine-headed Hydra: the endless decisions and distractions, the land mines of regret, the quicksand of nostalgia, the feeling it will never be done. Hard to face alone. Someone else's encouragement can make all the difference.

When my mother was about seventy, she and my stepfather moved from a large apartment to a small one in a senior living community. I went to Chicago to help her get ready for the move, which included sorting through the books and papers in her study. She was a serious writer and poet, though not well known. In her study were multiple copies of small-press books of her work, journals in which she had published poems, short stories, and essays, and files of correspondence with editors. The process of organizing it all was laced with sorrow that she had not gotten more recognition for her writing. The content of the work was often sad, too, about the losses in her life.

I was able to help my mother with the sorting decisions–to keep just one copy of each publication, for example, and to recycle much of the old correspondence with editors. More importantly, I cheered her on. I bore witness, with sincere enthusiasm, to the work she had done. We came across published poems I'd never seen, and I got her to read them aloud to me. She cried once, and that made me cry, too, so at least she wasn't crying alone. We also had fun. I read aloud to her the letters from editors praising her work, before we put them in the recycling. On a bookshelf, we lined up one copy of each journal, each anthology, each book in which she had work. What survived our sorting took up much less space than before, and this was the point. Still, when the publications were all side by side, it was impressive. "Look at all the work you've published!" I exclaimed. "People you don't even know have read it, all of it!"

My mother lived another fifteen years in the senior apartment building, a home she loved because of her view of Lake Michigan and because of her many friends in the building. By the time she died, she had pared down and beautifully organized her belongings. After her death, we found in her apartment a manila envelope for each of her children and grandchildren, labeled and containing loose photos of that person. Her example inspires me.

I found the following poem on her computer. (She liked to write doggerel as well as serious verse.)

In winter when the weather's bad
We don't feel old or frail or sad.
We just pursue our favorite sport
And sort and sort and sort and sort!
　　　–ALICE RYERSON HAYES

This could be the theme song for the Sorting Sisters. We've been getting to know each other in a tender way, as a side effect of sorting, though to call it a side effect is to understate the case. The sorting could be a side effect of getting to know each other.

Mary was working on the challenging task of organizing printed photos. Over several sessions, she reduced ten shoeboxes of random, loose photos to five, sorted by categories. When she mentioned that the box for "family" contained the photos of her late husband and her pets, I involuntarily laughed. Her Zoom face fell, and she said, "I didn't have any children, so my pets have been the closest thing to children."

"Of course. I don't know why I laughed," I said, remembering the sweet face of Mary's last dog, Doc Watson, who had died six months before. He was a member of the family, if there ever was one.

One day, Liz came to our midafternoon meeting with a flushed face. "I can't believe what I found!" She held up a small black metal ring and asked if we could guess what it was. "A buckle from a backpack?" I offered. No, it was the platinum aortic valve that had been in her father's heart when he died. She told us the story: She had taken care of her father when he was dying. After his body was cremated, she went to the crematorium to pick up his ashes. From a seat in the gallery, she watched through a plateglass window while a worker with one eye climbed into the oven to sweep up the bones and ashes. She asked him to look for the valve. "He sifted through the bones as carefully and gracefully as if his movements had been choreographed." Her voice broke when she said, "He was my father's last caregiver."

The man found the valve and gave it to her. It might seem strange, she said, but this little piece of metal meant a lot to her, and she always kept it on her desk. Then, a couple of years before, it had disappeared. She had looked everywhere. Thinking her cat might have knocked it onto the floor, she had even emptied out the vacuum cleaner bag and picked through the pile. Finally, sadly, she had given it up for lost.

Her project on this day was to clean off her desk, where she found, among other extraneous things, a small woven change purse from the Philippines. She was about to put it in the Goodwill giveaway box when . . . *Wait! What is this lump?* she wondered. It was the little platinum ring. "I must have put it there myself for safe-keeping and forgotten."

We all marveled at the story. It was an intimate story, and Liz got to share it with us. Without our group, her discovery might have been lonesome; she might never again have spoken, or even thought, of the dancer with the bones. And our hearts would not have been moved by the chronicle of the platinum aortic valve.

In the case of objects larger than aortic valves, objects that actually take up storage space, telling the story that goes with the object can sometimes make it possible to let the object go to its next, if not final, resting place. Once your friends have borne witness to the sentimental meaning of the object, it can take its last bow and retire from your home with dignity.

On a Saturday in early December, I lugged a big box of Christmas tree decorations down from the attic. When my children were growing up, they spent most Christmases with their father in Chicago, and my Christmases were lonely without them. Sometimes the kids and I decorated a tree in the living room before they went, and sometimes we did it after they came back, so I had a collection of decorations. Some had come down to me from my mother and even my grandmother. Some were made by my children.

Since I've become a grandmother, I've no longer been childless at Christmas. Either I have visited my grandchildren–along with their parents, whom I'm glad to see even if they are grown-ups–or they have visited me. At my house, they help me decorate the tree, and their noodle chains and paper stars have been added to the box. But this year, because of the pandemic, no grandchildren, neither mine nor my sister's, were going to show up at Christmas. The three old people in the house decided to dispense with a tree. The idea of passing on my Christmas tree decorations came to me in a sudden flash. I was exhilarated to realize how strong my letting-go muscles have become. It takes strength to hold on to things, and it takes even more strength to let them go. Wow! Could I really do this? I ascribe this strength to the Sorting Sisters.

I put the carton on the dining room table with two smaller cartons, one for each son's family, on either side. Then, as if dealing cards, I divided the decorations between the two boxes–a donkey here, a lamb there, a sleigh to Virginia, a Santa to Texas. Some angels with broken wings went into the wastebasket. When I reported back to my Sorting Sisters, I showed them a couple of my favorite decorations: a tiny antique church covered with snowy sparkles from Czechoslovakia that had hung on my grandmother's tree, and from my own childhood, a straw angel from Sweden, blowing a straw horn. I felt ready to say goodbye to them, put them into their respective boxes, and send them off in time to spend the coming Christmas in their new homes. As I told my friends, I felt unexpectedly liberated, not only from storing that particular cardboard box but from having to hold up that piece of family culture anymore. Now, along with the decorations, I can let go of the sadness about long-ago Christmases. If my grandchildren come to visit me at Christmas again, and I certainly hope they do, we can make cookies and hang them from the tree with yarn and eat them when Christmas is over, if Santa doesn't eat them first.

Admitting to some of the things you have kept can be embarrassing, and at the same time, learning about the strange things other people keep can be reassuring. It's a relief to find out that you're not the only one who has trouble letting things go.

One of us decided to clean out her refrigerator. You might think this is beside the point: Is this death-cleaning? But you wouldn't want to die with a smelly fridge, would you? She told us that she took out the chocolate Easter bunny that she had been keeping in the fridge for a long time, supposing that chocolate doesn't really go bad if you refrigerate it. As time passed, it had become a part of the refrigerator landscape and she hardly even saw it anymore. When she took it out, she looked at the "best by" date and discovered it was nineteen years old. She peeked under the foil and it didn't smell bad, but she took a great leap and disposed of it anyway, putting the foil covering into the bin with the cans, the chocolate into the compost. We applauded her.

Two of us who were going through file drawers on the same afternoon accumulated piles of empty old file folders with used labels on them: "astrological chart," "urgent correspondence," "chimney sweep info." We proudly showed our piles of empties to our friends on Zoom, and we both admitted that we thought of keeping them since "they might come in handy someday." (Whenever I hear myself using that phrase as the reason for keeping something, I try to make myself give it away.)

There are probably young people who have never even *seen* a file folder. My niece and her husband lived in my house for a few years, and I remember asking her when they moved in, "Where are your file cabinets?" "We don't have any file cabinets, "she said. "It's all digital." I was awestruck.

Even in my nondigital case, as I looked at my friend's pile of file folders, the veils fell from my eyes. It's not so hard to see that someone *else* doesn't need heaps of excess used file folders. Following on that revelation, I suddenly knew that I did not want a big pile of limp, dog-eared file folders. I put them in the recycling, though I will admit to keeping five of the crisper ones, just in case they might come in handy someday. Uh-oh.

It's natural for old people to reminisce about the past. I know that the noted German psychologist Erik Erikson came up with the concept of the life review process as an important developmental task for old people, believing that to accept and integrate the experiences of a lifetime, both positive and negative, is a natural way to prepare for death. I hadn't foreseen, however, that our Sorting Sisters group would be a place for reviewing and affirming our lives together.

One afternoon Nancy went through a box of old papers and note-books relating to her career as a social worker. She had given up that career years before we knew her to become a skillful and enthusiastic tree pruner, and her social worker days rarely came to her mind. Now, sorting through the social work box, she was moved as she remembered how hard she had worked and how much of her heart she had put into that life. She found a flyer for a program she had helped to develop for Kaiser Hospitals, making tattoo removal available to ex–gang members, to help them in seeking employment. I never would have guessed that Nancy knew about tattoo removal.

Another sorter took a break from her ongoing organizing of note-books from her teaching career to commit to an unusual project. For her, this, too, fell under the heading of death-cleaning. It was some-thing she wanted to bring to completion before she died. She would make a phone call that she had been putting off for a long time, to an ex-husband she had been estranged from and hadn't spoken to in years. She wanted to unravel a misunderstanding of some kind. She didn't know if she still had the right number for him, or if he would answer. It was a difficult call to make, but she knew that if she told us she was going to do it, she would. She returned to our midafternoon gathering to report that she had reached him, and they had talked, and both of them were glad of it. Clearing up an emotional misunderstanding is a kind of decluttering, too.

Over our months of sorting, we have each made significant prog-ress. We take pride, as a group, in each person's accomplishments. We admire the stack of neatly folded towels on their way to Goodwill, the gleaming oak of a desk surface, the orderly bookshelves where both books and ceramics are artfully displayed, the tidy medicine cabinet, the triumph of an empty cupboard shelf. An empty shelf is like money in the bank. You can save it until you need it.

We aren't finished. At our most recent meeting, Nancy–who came up with another good name for our group, the Stuffragettes–said she hopes she never finishes sorting because she doesn't ever want to stop meeting. It looks to me like there's no imminent danger of our finishing. As long as we have stuff, we Stuffragettes can sort it. We move in the direction of emptiness, but ultimate emptiness eludes us.

These days there are plenty of helpful books and websites about organizing, downsizing, and decluttering. The lesson of the Sorting Sisters is something different: The daunting task of organizing your stuff becomes easier when you do it in relationship with others. You can lighten your load and deepen your friendships at the same time.

I look forward to spending a Saturday afternoon now and then in solidarity with my Stuffragette friends, as we join together in the great struggle for freedom from clutter. It's a spiritual practice, and it takes us far beyond clutter and no-clutter. My life is enriched by the stories of the aortic valve and the flyer on tattoo removal. We honor each other's histories as they unfold, and we help each other discover what matters most to us in this moment. Together, we learn the elder's art of letting go. I love our meetings.

We sort not only to get ready to die but to get ready to live the life that remains to us. The less cluttered my house, the more I enjoy my life right now while I'm living in it. Of course, happiness is also possible in a house crowded with artifacts of the past, but what a pleasure it is to sit in an uncluttered room in my comfortable armchair with a cup of tea beside me on the otherwise empty side table, gazing raptly across the room at my orderly desktop, on which my stapler is clearly visible in case I need it.

And I still have boxes in the basement to attend to, so I still need my Sorting Sisters.

Sentient Beings Are Numberless, I Vow to Save Them

THE ODDS LOOK bleak for life on planet Earth. I'm grateful to Zen practice for training me to forget the odds and attempt the impossible. For forty-five years I've been chanting what we Zen practitioners call "the bodhisattva vows" at every Zen service:

Sentient beings are numberless, I vow to save them.
Delusions are inexhaustible, I vow to end them.
Dharma gates are boundless, I vow to enter them.
Buddha's way is unsurpassable, I vow to follow it.

A person who can vow to save all sentient beings can't quail at working for environmental, economic, and racial justice, can she? Even if she is old?

One of the most important things I can do as a white elder is to pay attention to what young people, Black and brown people, and others in circles beyond my own are doing for social justice. Paying attention is doing something. I speak here as a white person, with the limitations of a white person's point of view. These limitations are, by their very nature, mostly invisible to me, and paying attention is one way to remove the screens that block my vision.

Back in the sixties, we had some good ideas about how to make social change, but this is a different time, and we elders, even the savviest among us, are in a different phase of our lives–the last one. To be blunt, we're all going to be dead fairly soon. The Movement for Black Lives, the Green New Deal, the movement for LGBTQ rights, and the Sunrise Movement (with apologies to the many other important movements I'm unintentionally leaving out) were not created by old sixties activists. In my Zen life and my writing life, I can still be a teacher, but when the focus is on working for justice, it's my turn to learn from young people. So I open my eyes and pay attention. I bear witness to what I see. Then I can also stand up for them, and, since my time is short, pass on whatever I have that they find to be of use.

———

One Sunday morning in June 2020, not long after the murder of George Floyd, Francie and I walked around in downtown Oakland to see the murals that had blossomed on the storefronts. Many store windows had been boarded up when the businesses had to shut down because of the pandemic, or later, for protection during the protests. The big sheets of plywood made good canvases. In a spontaneous upwelling, hundreds of local artists came, along with school groups, youth groups, community groups. Contacted by word of mouth, by Black Lives Matter, by hashtags, they covered the plywood with black and brown faces and fists and flowers. They came first at night and then by day, to make art in the heart of the city.

Francie and I walked the quiet Sunday morning streets and the brightly colored murals called to us from either side. "George Floyd Lives Forever." "Justice for Breonna." "You tried to bury us, but you didn't know we were seeds." "Don't Kneel on Me," "Indigenous Peoples 4 Black Lives." George Floyd's face appeared again and again, along with Breonna Taylor's and many others, raging, grieving, dancing, rising up on the hard walls, painted in different strokes by different hands, on Fifteenth Street, on Broadway, on Webster, on Twelfth Street. Surely such a profusion of murals had never before appeared in the center of a city. A place for buying and selling had been transformed into a grassroots community art museum.

Two weeks before, I had seen on my computer screen the knee on the neck and, in the next moment, the knee *still* on the neck–*Oh god no, stop it, stop it*–and, incredibly, in the next moment, too, still there, still pressing down. Thank you, Darnella Frazier, seventeen years old, for your courage in bearing witness. *Bearing* is the word, for you bore witness to what must have been almost impossible to bear.

At the time of his murder, George Floyd was on a street in Minneapolis, two thousand miles away from me. Now it seemed that I was on the same street as George Floyd, in downtown Oakland. He was close to me because of what people in Oakland had spontaneously given: the plywood and paint, the labor and the ladders, the passion for justice. George Floyd looked directly at me. He asked me to look back at him, and I did.

Something big was happening in downtown Oakland, Mr. Jones, and Francie and I, two silver-haired white women, were finding out what it was. We were crying and calling out words to each other, like *amazing* and *miracle*–words inadequate to the largeness of what we felt.

———

What can old people do that's appropriate to their age? Or more particularly, what can *this* old person do that's appropriate to my age? I can do a lot of the same things I used to do, only slower. I can espouse the same causes but not do the heavy lifting. I can go to the demonstration but stay in the shade at the back of the plaza and leave early. It's good to keep showing up. When I was young, I was encouraged when I saw old people at marches and demonstrations. If and when I'm too frail to show up physically, I can keep on writing letters, making phone calls, and giving money as I'm able. As an experienced editor, I can help with putting together literature for various causes, though I may need some tech support along the way. When a junior high school student wants to interview me about my experience in the civil rights movement for a school project, as has happened a few times, I can make real for them some history–like gunshots fired on a hot night in Mississippi into a circle of people singing– that happened long before they and even their parents were born.

All of these activities are good. They make sense. They are logical steps on a path that points to justice. I will continue to join in such activities as I am able. But what I want to speak about here is not doing the same things more slowly. These days I find myself stepping off the linear path. I'm not following a map anymore.

———

I was very young when I went to Mississippi in the summer of 1964, as a volunteer with the Student Nonviolent Coordinating Committee (SNCC), to work on voter registration. It was scary to go, because three SNCC civil rights workers were murdered the week before I left for Mississippi. But the civil rights movement seemed like the most important thing that was happening, and to some extent, my youth protected me from understanding that I could die.

I thought that privileged white people like me should help Black people get their rights. That was a limited view. Once I got to Mississippi, I saw how much worse things were for Black people than I had ever imagined– and how much more risk they faced than I did. I only registered a few voters. My visible presence as a white woman put the lives of the Black couple who housed me in danger every time I walked in or out of their door. The "help" I gave to the movement was essentially in the form of bearing witness: writing an article for a hometown newspaper and telling white people back home what I had seen. But what I received was immeasurable: the experience of being part of a "beloved community" of people working together, risking their lives, and sharing their courage for the sake of freedom. I learned then that change comes only when people work together. When the Voting Rights Act was passed in 1965, I was glad that I had had a part, though a very small one, in an important achievement. I thought that Black people were really getting their freedom.

I was active in the women's movement and the antinuclear movement. I was arrested multiple times for civil disobedience. In recent years I worked in electoral politics, in getting out the vote for candidates I believe in. All this time I've operated on the assumption that we human beings can make things better. Sometimes, I admit, I'm not so sure about this anymore. How free have Black people gotten so far? Look what's happening to voting rights! As for the climate crisis, it's getting worse faster than it's getting better.

But we don't know what will happen. Sometimes positive surprises happen. Juneteenth, the day that enslaved people in Texas belatedly learned that they were free and had *been* free for two years, has recently been made a federal holiday. It may be a symbolic gesture recognizing a day with a complex history, but symbols matter, and the fact that all of our senators and almost all of our representatives felt they had to vote for it may signal a change in the wind.

Backward and forward have lost their meaning. It's not about a straight line anymore. The Movement for Black Lives, the Native American water protectors, the young Sunrise Movement—they don't move in straight lines. They spring up all over the place like geysers, they move in circles, they wheel around hubs. It's not logical sequencing that's going to save us.

I was a curious child. Earlier in these pages I told the story of how I got myself lost on purpose by wandering in circles beyond my neighborhood. I wanted to know what it feels like to be lost. Now again, I'm willing to wander off the map, to go in circles instead of straight lines, curious about what I'll discover. I'm working at letting go of my assumptions.

———

I've been talking with some white elder friends who are looking hard at their privilege and thinking about their legacies, whether in the form of investments or real estate or simply family history. They are entering into dialogue with Native people, African Americans, and others whose ancestors were robbed or enslaved or massacred by their ancestors.

My friend Louise Dunlap is one of these. She and her sisters inherited a piece of oak woodland in Northern California that had been in her father's family since the 1850s. When I first met Louise about twenty years ago, she was going on many peace walks with Native Americans and Buddhist monks and nuns—walks that acknowledged historical harm and honored sacred sites. She inspired me to go on some of those walks, too. Now that she's over eighty, joint trouble keeps her from walking much, and she has been focusing her attention on this piece of land and its original owners, learning her ancestors' role in the genocide and enslavement that took place in California and beyond. She has a book forthcoming about this history and what it means to her.

"When I was younger," she told me, "I wanted to be involved with every issue: nuclear, climate, racism, all the issues where we went wrong. Now I am working on what seems to me to be at the center of it all—trying to heal the colonizer mind. What can heal the world? How do I heal the mess my ancestors made? That's my project now."

I'll tell you something. I have ancestors who were enslavers. It's time for me to investigate this piece of family history. I have some family papers in the attic, and I'm finding my way to other papers in historical libraries. The past is not over; it's here in the present, and so is the future. Louise continues to inspire me. She reminds me that property isn't the only thing we pass on. If we're white, we need to challenge our old thought patterns in order not to pass on what I'm learning to call "colonizing mind." Those of us with property to leave behind can consider how to bring the idea of healing to that part of our legacy, and even if we don't have significant property, we can bring to light what we learn about the history of our ancestors, whether of harm or healing, hurting or being hurt. The history we pass on could play a part in future reconciliation. I want to enter this shadowed history while I still have time. I will be walking into unknown territory. I don't know where I will go. As I consider my part in this lineage, I will continue to listen to Black people. Going forward includes looking back.

———

A Zen koan asks, "What was your original face before your parents were born?" The old Zen master who poses the question is asking me to investigate my deepest, truest nature. He is not speaking of my great-great-great-grandfather, the one who belonged to the last generation of people in this country who "owned" human beings. He is not asking me what that man's face looked like. Still, looking for my face before my parents were born, I follow a fraying thread to a copy of that ancestor's portrait, in a cardboard box in the attic. I look at his face—he's young; he died at thirty-four. A high brow, a long nose, steady eyes. These are not my features, but could this be my original face? What part of my own true nature is to be found here? I have some exploring to do. There are some old letters waiting for me in the box.

———

I'm excited and a little nervous to be walking into unknown territory at the age of seventy-eight. I don't know who I will meet, but whether they are dead or alive, I will do my best to listen to what they have to say. I will be guided by young people who are asking me to widen my vision and step out of my comfort zone. I have faith that I won't be making this journey alone.

The Great Matter

ONE OF THE most important spiritual teachers in my life was, unexpectedly, an old Catholic priest, an elder if there ever was one.

A week after Easter, more than twenty years ago, my friend Fanny drove me up a country road outside of the town of Sonoma to meet Father Dunstan Morrissey in his "hermitage." At the entrance gate, two signs were swinging gently in the wind. One said Sky Farm, and the other, hanging below it:

> WAKE UP!
> LIFE IS TRANSIENT
> SWIFTLY PASSING
> BE AWARE OF
> THE GREAT MATTER
> DON'T WASTE TIME!

I recognized with surprise the words traditionally written on the han, the wooden board that is struck with a mallet to call Zen monks to zazen. I had been practicing Zen for twenty years and I was still looking for the Great Matter. You could also call it God. That looking had brought me to this gate.

When I was a child, I wanted to believe in God, but I didn't know how to go about it. What did "believe in God" really mean, anyway? My secular, anticlerical parents were no help.

I thought God might help me with the longing I felt and couldn't explain. I remember lying in the hammock on Grandma's screened porch, watching the rabbits hop on the dewy meadow behind her house on summer evenings, making magically long shadows. Nothing was wrong and yet the rabbits on the grass tore at my heart with each creak of the hammock, and I couldn't understand why the last light made me so sad. If I had believed that God was there watching us–me and the rabbits–everything might have been okay.

Years later, as a young adult, I heard Alan Watts and Ram Dass on the radio, talking about transcendence through meditation. When I first went to the Berkeley Zen Center to try it out, I hoped I would rise above my separate self to a place where I could see that everything was connected.

I loved the smell of tatami and incense, the *Heart Sutra* encouraged me ("The mind is no hindrance"), and Dogen opened up the view ("The whole moon and the entire sky are reflected in a drop of dew in the grass"). But zazen was hard for me. More difficult than the physical pain of staying still in a cross-legged position was the mental pain. I was comforted by the simple pull of gravity, and I noticed, and was grateful for, the breath that kept going in and out. But sometimes I felt trapped in my own mind. When I fell into bouts of depression or loneliness, as I did from time to time, I wanted someone I could call out to. *HELP ME! HELP ME!* I loved the dharma, but I didn't think the dharma could hear me calling.

At Sky Farm, Fanny parked beside the chapel, and we found Dunstan outside. He greeted us warmly, crinkling his eyes and laughing softly. He was a striking man in his late sixties, with white hair and a white beard. Over his robust belly he wore a French artist's smock of blue denim that made his blue eyes bluer.

He led us to a grassy slope beneath an oak. Beaming, he lifted a slab of plywood to reveal a deep coffin-sized hole in the dark dirt. "It came to me during my Easter retreat to dig my grave," he said. We stood together, the three of us, noticing we were alive, peering down into the hole and out at the lupine-blue view over the valley. I thought of the sign at the gate. *Life is swiftly passing. Wake up!*

Dunstan showed us the chapel and two guest cabins made of giant wine casks discarded by a local winery. These were fairy-tale chambers: twelve feet in diameter, with cone-shaped roofs like Vietnamese hats. I went inside one and right away I wanted to stay in the round room smelling of wine, to sleep in the single monk's bed, to sit at the wooden desk and look out the window at the rocky outcroppings on the opposite hill. I wanted to pick up the book beside the bed–*The Cloud of Unknowing*. An oak tree clicked its leaves in the breeze outside. A photograph of Gandhi hung on the wall. This would be a good place to look for God.

And so a few weeks later, I came back for my first retreat at Sky Farm. Dunstan invited me to come to Lauds in the chapel in the morning, and I said yes, not knowing what that was. At sunrise (I learned later he checked the time every day in *The Farmers' Almanac*) Dunstan rang the Angelus, the call to morning prayer, on a big iron bell mounted on a post beside the chapel. I crossed the dewy grass, saw Dunstan's worn old shoes outside the chapel door, and left mine there as well.

A window on the east side was made of one large piece of stained glass with abstract red flames. When the sun rose, its rays came through the red glass like a blaze of fire, turning the inside of the chapel a glowing red. It's strange how sensory stimuli produce such an effect of the sacred: the incense burning in copper boxes on the wall mixing its smell with the smell of wine; the gradual, pulsing increase of the morning light in the dark space; the candlelight reflecting on the gold paint on Mary's face in the icon painting.

I don't remember which psalms we chanted that first time, but I remember feeling held by the round walls of the chapel and by the words themselves. The sounds that came from our two mouths merged and curled around the round walls. God was apparently there even though I couldn't see him, and I was invited to join in praising him. Or her.

That I was welcomed to Sky Farm without question by this old Catholic man; that I was not asked, "What do you think you're doing here?"; that I didn't have to promise I believed in something; that the two of us stood in the rosy glow, connected in our chanting—not one, not two; all this was like a miracle but simpler than that—as simple as stepping over a threshold.

I came back to Sky Farm many times. Sometimes for a day, sometimes for a week, as if I could hear the call of the Angelus fifty miles away in Berkeley.

In the mornings I met Dunstan across the slab of his library table that was piled with books and papers. When it was cold, he built a fire in the woodstove. His giant Irish wolfhound Sophie (named for Sofia, Divine Wisdom, in the Russian Orthodox Church), thumped her tail on the floor. He made us green tea, much too strong, and he read aloud to me from whatever he was reading—Isaac the Syrian, Edith Stein—sometimes pausing for so long that I thought he was stopping, but it turned out he was resting his voice. This was our version of *lectio divina*, the Benedictine tradition of daily reading and contemplation of sacred texts.

He told me stories of his life, too, like how a book by Simone Weil mysteriously fell off a shelf into his hand in a secondhand bookstore when he was twenty and changed the course of his life and how, years later, he learned that the book had not been published by that date. He couldn't explain it and didn't try—it had happened. He spoke of being a hermit on the island of Martinique for a couple of years and of the voodoo priest who came by to tell him of Kennedy's assassination.

He often laughed, with a silent shaking of the shoulders, in the middle of his own sentences, and sometimes I knew why and sometimes I didn't. Sometimes it turned out he wasn't laughing, he was crying. Both the laughing and the crying meant he was moved by the story he was telling, the person he was remembering, the kindness that had been shown to him.

He spoke often of "the realm beyond the opposites," something akin to Buddhist emptiness. I told him that the Buddhist teaching of emptiness was scary to me—I wanted something to hold on to. He pulled Simone Weil's *Gravity and Grace* off the shelf and read to me: "Grace fills empty spaces, but it can only enter where there is a void to receive it, and it is grace itself which makes this void."

When I talked to him about my personal life—my concerns for my mother, my delight in my adult sons, a failed romance—he listened and responded in mysterious, philosophical ways. Never "Why don't you call him up and ask to talk it over with him?" but something more like, "God shows us how deep the well of our love goes." It was as if I spoke to him in one language and he answered me in another, and yet I felt heard and comforted.

Sometimes, when Dunstan was away, I stayed in the main house at Sky Farm to take care of Sophie. One night a wild winter storm shook the house, the wind howled, the rain pounded, I heard crashing of branches, and the electricity went out. Sophie and I were alone there, and I was afraid and excited, and grateful that Sophie was with me. I was in the place Dunstan had made, a place where Dunstan's God lived. I prayed, not asking for anything in particular, feeling alive in the great maw of the universe, as if my ribs were torn open like branches in order for my heart to spread out.

A few years after I met him, Dunstan had a stroke. I wasn't there, but he told me he got up to ring the Angelus bell and on the way, he felt dizzy and had to get down on the ground. He managed to crawl across the grass and ring the bell, and a visitor coming to Lauds took him to the hospital, where he stayed for a week or so.

After he got home, he needed extra help for a while. I took a turn, staying at Sky Farm for a couple of weeks, and I cooked for him and drove him on errands.

I remember thinking that he was the only person I loved purely, wanting his happiness without wondering what I would get back from him and without all the hopes and worries that are inevitably mixed in with the other loves I feel, like the love I feel for my children and grandchildren. Those loves are huge–they couldn't be huger–but they aren't completely pure.

Dunstan loved me, too. I was one of many people he loved, and one of many who loved him. He was the hub of an invisible wheel of spiritual friends, a mentor to remarkable people all over the world who sometimes turned up at Sky Farm and with whom he kept up a copious correspondence. At home in Berkeley, I received a constant stream of photocopied articles in the mail, and three-by-five-inch index cards with quotes typed out for me on his ancient Underwood typewriter, and religious books he'd ordered from catalogs. These readings were always just what I needed at the time.

This mutual unconditional love had something to do with God. I was searching for God and I found Dunstan. As an old white man with a white beard, he even looked a lot like God–one version of God. I didn't actually think Dunstan *was* God, but when I was with him, I felt close to God. And I began to see that God and Buddha had nothing against each other. They got along well.

In 2000, Dunstan invited me to move to Sky Farm. I had spoken to him of my idea of experimenting with living somewhere other than my old

Berkeley house. After the stroke, the stairs in the house at Sky Farm had become difficult for Dunstan, and he had had a little apartment built for himself as an addition to the library. The now-empty main house could be my quarters.

Thinking about what to do, I walked into the chapel by myself one morning and it was flooded with that red light. I said to myself, *I'm entering the home of my heart. I'm entering the heart of my home.* So I said yes, and I rented out my house in Berkeley.

This was a decision I made wholeheartedly, willing not to know, ready to take the leap into a new life. It felt wonderful to "shoot the hoop," as a friend calls it, without waffling, ready for whatever would unfold.

A few days before I was to move in, Dunstan called me. "Susan," he said, "I'm sorry to tell you this. The house burned down yesterday. The stone statue of St. Joseph that stood by the front door–it's the only thing that didn't burn. St. Joseph stands alone among the ashes." His voice broke for a moment, and I knew that his tears were not tears of grief for the house that was gone but tears of gratitude for the saint who refused to burn. "I'm fine," he continued. "Naked I came into this world, and naked I'll leave it. You're the one I worry about. I have my little apartment."

I felt suddenly stripped, too, unencumbered by expectations and yet full of faith. I felt that I had been shot from a cannon, and even as I held the receiver in my hand, I was spinning in the vast blue sky, floating beyond gravity, beyond the realm of the opposites. I could look down at my small self and know that I would be all right, that the next thing would happen, whatever it was. In that moment I was free, both grief-stricken and joyful but not afraid.

Seeing Sky Farm was terrible, though. The statue of St. Joseph stood in a black field of twisted metal and ash. Charred book pages lifted and flapped like moths above blackened pot lids, ceramic shards, the skeleton of–was it the stove?

With Dunstan's encouragement, I moved into one of the wine barrels. It was a lot smaller than the house, but I loved my cell. The essentials were there, and I was happy. I kept on looking for God, without desperation now, and with Buddha's support. On the days I didn't drive to work in Berkeley, Dunstan and I had our talks in the library. I often cooked lunch for him.

Dunstan knew about Buddhism. He had sat sesshins with Shunryu Suzuki Roshi in San Francisco, and he kept a framed photograph of him on a bookshelf. He'd also been to several meditation retreats in the tradition of S. N. Goenka, pioneer of vipassana meditation in modern times, and his library included many Buddhist books. For my sake, he instituted a second service in the chapel in the late afternoons, to chant the *Heart Sutra*, which he magically produced on stiff chant cards, written in Chinese characters with an English translation underneath. He came to this afternoon chapel service in his bathrobe and went to bed soon after. (He rose daily at 2:00 or 3:00 a.m.)

But alas, in the realm on this side of the opposites, life in the wine barrel was not sustainable. I had a bit of a walk up the hill to the bathroom and the kitchen, and I had no phone or internet. After a couple of months, grateful for having actually *lived* at Sky Farm, I moved out. I didn't lose Dunstan, though. Not yet. I came back often.

In Zen we say the teachers and the teachings are like the finger pointing at the moon and the moon is enlightenment. We are told not to mistake the finger for the moon. Dunstan was the finger pointing at the moon of God.

At the end of Lauds every morning, Dunstan ceremoniously faced each of the four directions, then earthward, then heavenward. At the last, he extended his arms above him–ten fingers pointing. God was in every direction. I, standing beside him in the chapel, still didn't exactly *see* God for myself, but I knew I was looking in the right direction. There wasn't a wrong one.

———

When Dunstan died a few years ago, I felt that I had lost not only a beloved teacher but also my best connection to God. Now I have to keep searching without Dunstan's help.

I've come to realize that seeking God is not like hunting for your car keys: when you find the keys, you stop your fishing around. But God is with me only as long as I keep on looking, and the moment I stop, I've lost God again. In Zen we say, "Inquiry and response come up together."

So I keep on practicing Zen, reading Dogen, meditating, and searching for the one who dwells in the realm beyond the opposites. I wonder: *To what other surprising places will the looking still take me?* Maybe God is that which can't be found. That's okay, because God is in the looking.

Today I put on my altar one of the three-by-five-inch cards Dunstan sent me, this one with a quotation from Meister Eckhart.

Whoever would enter God's ground, His inmost part, must first enter his own ground, his inmost part, for none can know God who does not first know himself.

I haven't lost Dunstan after all. He's still with me, pointing in every direction.

Tears

IUSED TO CRY easily, but in recent years I lost my tears. When people I loved died, I hardly cried. Loss knocked the breath out of me and I was shrouded in woe, as if I were dead myself rather than a mourner at the graveside.

I connect this drought of tears to two things: taking an antidepressant and aging. I'll come to the aging later. I started taking Zoloft twenty years ago, when I was suffering from a severe depression, an experience I've written about before. I was a wraith, becoming substantial only when connected to another person. The antidepressant revived me, making me feel not drugged but normal. It was not that something extra was added but that obstructions were removed—a weight lifted, a tight belt loosened, windows no longer painted shut. I found the ground again under my feet and went on with my life, making, doing, studying Zen, teaching, loving as best I could. I still struggled with loneliness, but that was my way, beyond the reach of Zoloft. I worried about the planet, but who didn't? I certainly didn't expect Zoloft to fix that. The first time I started on Zoloft was long enough ago that I don't remember now whether it made me stop crying, but the main thing was, I was myself again, putting one foot approximately in front of the other.

It bothered me, though, that it was a tiny blue pill that made my life seem livable. It felt like cheating. Okay, granted, if I were diabetic I wouldn't refuse insulin, but this was different. In this case, you couldn't measure my blood chemistry and find something real that was missing. I berated myself: if I were stronger and braver, a true Zen practitioner, I would be able to face life's difficulties all by myself. Characteristically hard on myself, I didn't feel this way about other people who were taking antidepressants. I knew *they* weren't cheating. After a couple of years, thinking I'd gotten the leg up I needed and was now stable, I went off Zoloft, carefully, gradually.

It took a year or so for the depression to come back–the slippery slope, the quicksand sucking at me. My despondency wasn't situational. The personal circumstances that most distressed me–no partner, my children and siblings living far away–were no worse than when I had been on Zoloft, but the void that threatened to erase me was gaping open again. I went back to the little blue pill.

A few years went by, grandchildren got born, books got written, body parts were replaced. And again I thought, *I'm okay now, I don't need this crutch anymore.* I went off Zoloft for the second time, and guess what? After a couple of years, the same thing happened. The slipping and sliding.

So, for the third time, I returned to the fold. This time the transition was rocky, the anxiety intense, and I went through a couple of weeks of wanting to jump out of my skin. I wouldn't have stuck it out if I hadn't already experienced Z's benefits. When I finally steadied and found solid ground again, I said to myself, *Okay, this is myself. I'm not cheating. This is what I need to do to keep from being sucked down into the gray sludge. This is me, getting my serotonin levels back to normal. The little blue pill is no big deal, simply the smallest child in the ordinary family of vitamin pills that wait together each day in a row of plastic nests, S-M-T-W-T-F-S, to be swallowed.* I let go at last of a sense of shame. That was quite a few years ago.

As I get older, more people I love keep dying, and I have been missing my tears. Reading about children separated from their parents at the border, I felt a constriction in my chest, but no tears came. On YouTube, I watched huge chunks of arctic glaciers fall into the sea, and not one drop fell from my eye. I felt grief, for sure, but it hardened to concrete inside me. I don't know how else to talk about this except with imperfect metaphors.

I admit to feeling a "flattening of affect," something I have heard people complain about in connection with antidepressants. It's an apt expression, because the phrase itself lacks any feeling. Sometimes I have even wondered if Zoloft is bad for my creativity. I don't know.

I have missed *lacrimae rerum*–"the tears of things," the tears of the world. The phrase comes from Virgil's *Aeneid*. As Aeneas looks at a temple mural of the Trojan War, depicting his ancestors killing and being killed, he is moved to say "*Sunt lacrimae rerum.*" Because of the ambiguity in the Latin grammar, the sentence can be variously understood as, "There are tears of things," "There are tears in things," or "There are tears for things." It is unclear whether the tears are the tears of humans as they regard the world or whether the world itself is doing the weeping. Perhaps Virgil meant it to be both. I like poet Seamus Heaney's translation, "There are tears at the heart of things." I wanted to weep along with the world.

I consulted a psychopharmacologist about my dry eyes, and he suggested taking just half a Zoloft. A simple, radical idea. I thought about it for a couple of weeks, as I remained tearless in the face of the pandemic, the loss of life and livelihood around the world, George Floyd's murder by police, my own painful separation from faraway loved ones. I decided to try. And if I had to go back from half a tiny blue pill to a whole tiny blue pill, it wouldn't be such a shock to my system.

At the kitchen table one morning, as I was taking my vitamin pills, I told Francie and Bob that I was going down to half a pill in the hope of finding my way to tears. I wanted them to be my witnesses and to be ready for changes.

One day, at the same breakfast table, I said, "It's been two weeks now that I've been taking half a Zoloft."

"Is it working?" asked Francie.

"I think I feel at least a little bit sadder," I said hopefully.

We burst out laughing.

Months have gone by. Months of continuing pandemic. Months in which police have continued to kill unarmed Black people, months of lies from our government, and in the last weeks, an inferno of fire on the West Coast, with smoke causing a double imprisonment.

I am crying again, not a lot, but a little. Maybe I'll get better at it. What is the strange arithmetic of my tears? How many acres have to burn for me to collect a teaspoon? How many species have to go extinct for a tablespoon? It's not to be measured. Each salty drop reminds me that I'm human, that I'm responsive.

In my experience, there's a difference between being depressed and being sad. Depression is self-referential. It takes things personally: *I don't belong anywhere. There's something wrong with me. I'm alone because I don't know how to love.* One reason it's so depressing to be depressed is that you can't stop thinking about your miserable self. Sad, on the other hand, is how you feel when a goldfinch crashes into your window and breaks its neck. When your father goes blind from detached retina. Sadness connects you to the little bird, to your blind father. And tears bring you even closer.

I'm not saying it's great when a bird breaks its neck on the window because that gives me the opportunity to cry. I'm saying that when sad things happen, as they reliably do, crying makes me less separate. This morning I read that "parents of 545 kids separated at the border still haven't been found." In a photo, a crying toddler clings to his mother's leg while her palms are flat on the roof of a car and she is being patted down by a guard. The child's twisted-up, tear-streaked face makes me cry. He gets mixed up with my children and my grandchildren; I feel the hands of the guard on my thighs. My crying doesn't directly help the toddler, but it moves me toward him. His tears call forth my tears, like the moon pulling on the tides.

What are tears for, anyway? Zoologists have said that other animals cry tears to lubricate their eyes—as humans do when chopping onions, for example—but humans are the only animals whose eyes produce tears for emotional reasons. (This is now disputed by some.) Other animal babies whimper and cry out in distress when separated from their mothers, as human babies do, but only human babies make tears along with their wailing. Tears are fundamentally human. When I cry, I feel like I'm in solidarity with all human beings. *Homo lacrimosus.* It is possible, however, that you can be a loving human without crying.

Darwin didn't know why people cry. He thought it was a useless trait from the standpoint of survival. Now some scientists believe that weeping is a form of communication, a defense against aggression, an encouragement of altruism. Tears elicit an innate response that connects us.

When I was a very young child, my mother and I lived alone while my father was away in the army, and it frightened me to see her cry. I didn't have words or even distinct thoughts about it, but a gut reaction. She was supposed to make the world safe for me—there was no one else around to do it—and she was not supposed to be hurt or grieving. When I was a little older but still a child, if any of my younger siblings cried, I felt sad but not afraid. I wanted to comfort them if I could.

When I was a teenager, it still upset me to see my mother cry. My life didn't depend on her quite the way it had when I was two, but seeing a parent cry is distressing at any age. I remember my mother fleeing the dinner table in a sudden burst of tears because my father teased her for lighting up a corncob pipe instead of a cigarette, to go with her after-dinner coffee. It sounds like a funny incident, but it wasn't. She had bought the pipe in a smoke shop in Harvard Square as a creative device to use during one of her many attempts to quit smoking. (She didn't quit that time, but she did manage to quit about ten years later.) "That makes you look ridiculous," my father said, "like some old codger from Kentucky." My mother pushed back her chair as her tears came, and my little sisters and I sat at the table in shocked silence, listening to her footsteps running up the stairs.

When you see tears on another person's cheeks, you feel compassion whether you want to or not, and you instinctively want to help them, as I did with my siblings. When my ex-husband and I were having a fight and I started to cry, it became harder for him to continue the fight. I didn't cry as a manipulation—it came quite naturally to me; though my tears did not resolve our differences, they brought about a temporary cease-fire.

I didn't see my father cry until he became blind in old age after both his retinas detached. His blindness taught him, willy-nilly, to be vulnerable. He allowed people to get closer to him because he had to. He cried when I gave him a braille pocket watch for a present, the first time I visited him as a blind man, and I cried, too, though he couldn't see my tears. Those tears brought us as close as I'd ever felt to him. We might as well have been shedding each other's tears.

Crying is gendered behavior in the European-American culture I grew up in. Women cry more than men. Here is some information about crying that made me laugh, which I found on the internet. I share it here in case you find it useful.

"According to the German Society of Ophthalmology, which has collated different scientific studies on crying, the average woman cries between 30 and 64 times a year, and the average man cries between 6 and 17 times a year. Men tend to cry for between two and four minutes, and women cry for about six minutes. Crying turns into sobbing for women in 65 percent of cases, compared to just 6 percent for men." I can't help picturing a researcher sitting next to the weeper with a stopwatch. Or are people timing themselves and self-reporting the change to sobbing?

Tears have unexpected priorities. How strangely easy it is to cry in the movies, for people who don't even exist. I have perplexed myself by crying when an imaginary child's imaginary dog dies an imaginary death on a screen of pixels, and yet I have had no tears when someone I truly love has truly died. Perhaps these movie tears serve to keep the tears ducts open and generally lubricate compassion in a safe way. The grief ends when the movie ends. Perhaps the weeping is displaced from personal experiences of deep sorrow.

Research shows that as we get older, if we are women, we cry less, even if we're not taking Zoloft. And when we do cry, our crying gets quieter. Rarely do noises accompany the tears. Men cry less, too–until they get into their seventies, when they start to cry more than they used to. I gather this from anecdotal evidence on the internet and anecdotal evidence from my own life, like my blind father, who couldn't see out of his eyes but could cry out of them. Winston Churchill, that great war hero, was famous for shedding tears on state occasions of much gravity during his second term as prime minister, when he was in his late seventies.

I have no data on this, but it seems to me that old men don't care as much about being tough as they did in their youth. I like to think that gender differences are modulated in old age. Old people become more gender fluid, in both appearance and intention, though I have not researched this theory. Old men tend to have softer hearts and softer skin than young ones. Women's bodies drift toward the amorphous in shape. People don't generally care as much what other people think of them when they are old.

Another thing that changes as we age is the reason for our tears. If someone hurts my feelings, if something I love is taken from me, or if I'm tangled in a web of incorrect computer passwords, I may well be upset, but these things don't make me cry much anymore. Perhaps we old ones have cried enough for ourselves, for our betrayals and disappointments in love and work. Enough. Now those of us who have survived to old age and have food and shelter are better able to turn our gaze away from ourselves and cry for others who are hurt or helpless. *Lacrimae rerum.* Tears of the world.

Certain things always make me cry, at any age and at any serotonin level–like a group of small children singing together–and I hope they always will.

Witnessing beauty in nature makes me cry, especially when it's unexpected or unusual. Like the time I stood with some friends in a field behind our motel in Casper, Wyoming, in 2017, while the moon passed directly in front of the sun, and we were drenched for almost three minutes in a dark yellow light I'd never seen before.

Seeing people reaching out to each other in love makes me cry. Take the time I was waiting to meet a friend at the International Terminal of San Francisco Airport and the passengers on a flight from China were coming out of customs. A woman came through the swinging doors carrying a swaddled baby, and I saw her look around at all the people waiting in the lobby and zero in on a young couple with searching eyes who held a sign with a name on it, and I saw her pass the baby into their outstretched arms.

My female animal body has excreted all kinds of fluids over the course of my life: drool, piss, tears, snot, blood, and milk, in roughly chronological order of appearance. I now no longer excrete either blood or milk in the natural course of things, but most of the rest continue, and as the years go by, I may come full circle back to drool, though I hope not. I do hope the crying continues, but I understand that the quantity of tears is meaningless. It's the feeling that counts. It's okay not to shed tears, but it's not okay to deny the sadness or refuse the connection with the suffering of others.

Tears connect me to others. Even when I cry alone over a personal sorrow, the weeping reminds me that I am a human body, one member of a species that cries. Oscar Wilde said, "Though my heart is broken, hearts are made to be broken: that is why God sends sorrow into the world." The tears themselves are not the point, but they are a sign of compassion, which *is* the point, and I welcome them.

Meeting the Final Deadline

WE HUMANS could be the only species who are lucky enough to know we are going to die. I say lucky because this knowledge makes life shine. A sign I made hangs over my desk:

DON'T THINK FOR A MOMENT
YOU'RE NOT GOING TO DIE.

Does this seem weird to you? Every time I happen to notice it, I wake up for a minute. I remember not only my approaching death but the happy corollary: *I'm not dead yet! I'm alive!*

I used to be afraid of death. Now, not so much. It's partly a side effect of getting old. It's not only me. Old people in general are, by their own reports, less afraid of death than young people. We have less to lose, and some of us are getting tired. As our aches and pains get worse, we may even look to death as a safe form of pain management.

At sixteen, I was old enough to drive. As a septuagenarian, I'm old enough to die. I don't *want* to die right now, but it wouldn't be a tragedy if I did. I've had a long turn on the swing. A lot of people I know have already done it, and even though I don't exactly expect to see them again, I'll be expressing my solidarity with them when I go. *If you can do it–Mary, Friedel, Molly–I can do it, too.* Dying is becoming a companionable thing to do.

I fear death less, but I think about it more. I can't help it; death urges itself upon me. In the last several years, the outbreak of death among close friends my own age has been painful. No matter how much I love them, I can't stop them from leaving. The generation ahead of me in my family–parents, aunts, and uncles–is all gone, and I'm the oldest of four siblings. I'm on the cutting edge. I never volunteered for this front-line position and yet I feel I must summon the courage to look ahead at where we're all going.

At this writing I'm seventy-eight, five years older than my father was when he died of prostate cancer. You'd think it would be impossible to be older than your own father. My mother died in her eighties, so I have a few years before I catch up with her. Even though I'm healthy now, I'm going to die, and it could be sooner rather than later–sooner could be tomorrow, from an accident, or next month, from COVID-19. Later could be . . . Actually, at this point, how much of a gap can there be between sooner and later?

My fears now are not about what will happen to me after I die but about the difficulties on this side of death. My mother used to say, "The young fear death; the old fear dying."

I'm afraid I will die alone. But who knows? Maybe this is what I will want. You hear stories of people waiting until they are alone to die.

I'm afraid of dying in a lot of physical pain, or hanging on barely alive, hooked up to tubes in an ICU. I've done my best to address these things in my advance directive: yes to "making me comfortable," no to the tubes for life support. I'll get through it somehow. This is truly a case of "I'll cross that bridge when I come to it." Apparently, all human beings know how to die. I find it reassuring that everybody who's gone before me has managed it, and I trust that I'll be able to do it, too. I have no idea what dying will be like, so I tell myself: *Don't borrow trouble by worrying needlessly about problems that may never come up.*

I fear the pain of leaving, of being parted from loved ones. No way that's going to be easy, but if, along the way, I keep on telling people I love them and acting accordingly, this will make parting easier.

My biggest fear is that I won't be ready. It's a matter of timing. I fear dying too soon, before I've finished the sorting, before I've let go of all my lingering fears and regrets, before I understand that the life I've led has been just right, sorrows and all.

I'm studying death and practicing getting ready in various ways, like putting that sign over my desk. (Don't think for a moment you're not going to die!) I think I can do it–accept that I'm going to die, I mean. Day by day, I'm getting closer to accepting. Worst case scenario: at the end I'll just say, "Here I come, ready or not!"

Anne Aitken was a twentieth-century Zen practitioner and the wife of the Zen teacher Robert Aitken. She was a student of Master Yamada Koun. One day he asked her, "What do you think of death?"

She replied, "Why, it's like when a bus stops before you–you get on and go."

I want to be like her. I want to accept my death before I die.

I've been wondering about death all my life, ever since I realized that there was such a thing. It happened the summer I was five, when death came as a weasel in the night and stole the lives of our cat Purr's five newborn kittens, leaving their bloody and mangled bodies on the screened porch of our rented summer house, for five-year-old me to come upon in the morning. The carnage terrified me. And our dear Purr had disappeared. Later that day, my mother drove slowly along the country roads while I called out the open window, "Purr! Purr!" But we never saw her again. I understood that she had gone wild with grief.

In childhood it was the deaths of others that I feared, especially my parents'. This was in spite of the fact that a favorite game for us neighborhood kids was to hang around in the bushes of a vacant lot pretending we were orphans living in the woods, free at last of adult supervision. My own death was remote, ungraspable. Once, not long after the murderous weasel's visit, I had a nightmare in which my father leaned over to plug in the radio and he touched the socket in a way I had been taught not to do. He was instantly electrocuted right there in his orange armchair, going first rigid and then limp, like I'd seen in cartoons. The dream clung to my back for years, digging its claws into my shoulders.

When I was in seventh grade, the mother of my classmate Danny died of leukemia and I saw that death could come out of nowhere. There was no reason for leukemia to choose her, a nice mom I knew slightly from Danny's childhood birthday parties. The story was that she had discovered she had leukemia when the dentist noticed that her gums were unusually white. This was precisely the death-to-be-feared of a parent, terrible beyond speaking. I liked Danny, but I could say nothing to him. I could only look at him out of the corner of my eye, wondering how he managed to keep on walking and talking and doing his homework.

In adolescence, the idea that I, too, would die came into clearer focus. I remember a strange incident when I was fifteen and traveling in Europe with my family. In Paris one day, I stayed in the hotel with a stomach bug while the rest of the family went to the Bois de Boulogne. When I looked at myself in the bathroom mirror, my gums suddenly looked very white; I was sure I had leukemia. I didn't tell my parents because I wasn't *completely* sure, and not wanting to worry them prematurely, I suffered silently with this knowledge. I got over the stomach bug but not the leukemia. I wandered through Paris with my family in an altered state, seeing the fountains of the Tuileries, the *Mona Lisa*, the bookstalls through a veil of grief for my short life. The evening light reflected on the Seine was beautiful and fading.

A couple of days later, I looked furtively at the gums of my parents and siblings when they smiled or laughed and then again at my own gums in the hotel mirror. My gums were actually the same color as theirs! The feeling that I was soon to die died itself, unspoken, but the fact that I was indeed going to die some day–this fact I now believed, having lived for a couple of days with my own diagnosis of incurable leukemia.

When I became a mother, there was a new reason to be afraid of death. First one child and then another needed me for their survival. I was divorced when the kids were very young, and I had sole custody, so the fear intensified. Now I really couldn't die. I became phobic–I was afraid of flying, I was claustrophobic. Also, my children absolutely couldn't die, because nothing worse than that could be imagined. Children most fear the death of their parents and parents most fear the death of their children. As I realized anew that death could break the most precious connections in my life, it became even scarier.

What can a person do about fear of death?

We didn't have a religious practice in my family when I was a child, and there was no talk of what happened after you died, no talk of heaven or hell. Nevertheless, thanks partly to my Quaker grandmother, I developed a sense of god with a small g as I grew up. There was something much bigger than me that surrounded me. I adopted holy places in my childhood world: there was, in summer, a secret clearing in the tall bayberry bushes on the flank of a hill where I could lie on my back and watch the clouds travel; there was a little desk in a corner of my grandmother's attic with a view of the prairie, and on the desk there were boxes of ancient postcards whose smell connected me to the faraway and long-ago. I had a sense of the invisible beyond, something on the other side of those clouds, something in that box of postcards that comforted me. I don't know. When my son Sandy, age about four, asked me what would happen to him after he died, I told him god would take care of him. I wasn't lying. I did believe, and still do, that something huge would make a place for him, for everyone. This feeling helped me, but it's vague. I grew up with a fear of death in spite of it. I still wanted to know: What is death?!?

When my kids were little, I rang the doorbell at the Berkeley Zen Center, because of death. If I were immortal, I wouldn't have bothered. As it was, I hoped that Zen would show me the meaning of my life before it was over. I hoped it would help me overcome my fear of death and be ready to go when the time came.

I received zazen instruction in the attic zendo, under the eaves. I was told to "Sit still, count your breaths to ten and start again." That was a disappointment. How could such a tedious exercise be the path to understanding the meaning of life and death? But I hung around, attracted by the smell of the tatami mats and the *thwock thwock thwock* of the wooden fish drum as we chanted in the morning. It turned out there was a lot more to Zen than counting to ten.

Sitting in silence with others in the zendo, breathing with others, our one body sharing the air, gave me faith. Each sound born from quiet was particular: a slight cough, a creak of wood, the whisper of fabric moving against fabric as a leg was shifted, and after zazen, the nine full bows–nine soft drum rolls of all our knees thumping against the floor. In morning service, each strike on the big bell made sound waves distinct enough to count, spreading and fading like widening circles in water. My ears loved everything they heard. I don't know why, but the sounds gave me the gift of fearlessness, at least a little piece of it.

Every morning we chanted the *Heart Sutra*, and I memorized it right away so I could take it with me wherever I went. I have been glad ever since to have it in my pocket, as handy as a handkerchief, for all kinds of situations. Here's a good line, for example: "There is no old age and death and also no extinction of it." I didn't understand it then and still don't, but that doesn't stop it from helping me.

Somewhere along the way I learned the sad story of Kisagotami, the young woman who came to Buddha crazed with grief, her dead child in her arms, asking him for medicine to make her child well. She could not accept that her baby was dead. Buddha said he would help her if she brought him a mustard seed from a household that had not known death. She set off hopefully, knocking on doors, and each home had a mustard seed, but at every home, someone had died. People told her, "There are more dead than living in this family." She understood at last that everyone dies, including her child. She buried him in the forest and returned to Buddha to become one of his disciples, one of the first women ancestors. I doubt she ever completely stopped grieving, but I'm glad she found a path to follow and a way to help herself and others, including me.

Buddha taught that everything is impermanent and that fighting against this truth only makes things worse. Every single one of us is going to die, no matter how many parts we get replaced beforehand. Still, I wish that Kisagotami's child could have died later, *after* his mother instead of before.

There are lots of Zen stories about "the Great Matter" of birth-and-death, and I'm reassured that the old Zen masters considered death an urgent matter. Urgent and unknowable.

Not knowing is highly valued in Zen.

The (possibly apocryphal) story goes that a Samurai asked the eighteenth-century Zen Master Hakuin, "Where will you go after you die?"

Hakuin: "How am I supposed to know?"

Samurai: "You're a Zen master!"

Hakuin: "Yes, but not a dead one."

The more I consider death, approaching it from different angles, the more I realize that I can't know what it is. And the more this not-knowing becomes familiar, the less afraid I am. *There is no old-age-and-death and also no extinction of old-age-and-death.* Befriending my mortality is a work in progress, and it won't be done until . . . I die, of course.

I'm a list-maker, particularly of to-do lists: what I have to do today, or this week, or before I teach a class or take a trip. Even though I'm the one who makes the lists, the lists themselves often get the upper hand. These days I have a to-do list of things to accomplish before I die, not written down but in my head, like finishing writing projects, reconnecting with certain old friends, downsizing my material possessions, and sorting the boxes of photos in the attic. It's not a bucket list, not a list of fun adventures but of responsibilities. Aspiring to be a reliable person, how can I take time for the fun things until I finish my duties? Sometimes I feel as though I've spent the first three quarters of my life getting ready to live and now, instead of actually living, I'm spending the last quarter getting ready to die. What a waste!

I do finish things when I have a deadline, like this essay I'm writing—if you're reading it, that means I finished it—and for this reason I often create deadlines for myself in order to make myself get things done. But the downside of deadlines is deadline stress. I now feel a dull but constant deadline stress about the big deadline ahead, a deadline I did not create: the *dead* line. I can't get an extension on this one and yet I have the notion that I have to do everything on my list before I die. Is this what I think life is?

Get born
Learn to read and write
Make your to-do list on a really long piece of paper
Check each thing off one by one
Die

No! It's time to let go of the idea of checking everything off; time to practice accepting my life as it has been and is now. I'll do the best I can to get ready, and for my kids' and my siblings' sake, I'll keep on sorting, but I'll remember to be alive in the meantime. I'll die in the middle of something no matter what: a day, a breath, a visit with a friend, an essay. Something will not be finished. I might as well toss out the big to-do list and go to the beach, at least once in a while. I might as well be present in my life.

In any case, I will meet the dead line. I can't fail, no matter how many items are left on the list, because I will be right there meeting death when I die.

I used to love hiking in the mountains, when I could still walk long and far and high. Once, I was lying on my back on a big slab of granite at the edge of a stream, ten thousand feet above sea level. I was alone, or rather, I was the only human being around, having taken a little walk away from my companions at the campsite. I removed my boots and socks and reached one bare foot into the cold stream. The granite under me was warm from the sun. Out of the corner of my eye, the red of Indian paintbrush and the purple of lupine were waving back and forth, out of focus. I shielded my eyes to look across the meadow at a giant granite dome rising above me, polished by glaciers thousands of years ago; thousands of years hence, the dome would still be there, rising. The vastness of this place and time received my smallness and made me happy. I remember clearly the thought that suddenly came to me unbidden: *It would be okay if I died right now*. I was part of the mountain and the mountain was part of the planet and the planet was part of . . . you know what I mean. But I didn't die right then, and I was happy about that, too. I was happy to rejoin my friends at the campsite and cook up some red lentil soup for dinner.

Now I don't lie on boulders at high elevations, but I walk by the bay in Berkeley. Yesterday a friend and I were favored with the unusual sight of a seal appearing and disappearing just offshore. We stood in silence together, waiting for each reappearance, until it was too far away to see when it came up. Thank you, seal.

I take walks in the neighborhood, too, and on this crisp November afternoon, as I walked around the familiar block where I've lived for almost fifty years, I was astounded by the liquid amber tree just four doors down, its red leaves waving against the blue sky. Some leaves were spinning down to join the bright splashes already decorating the gray, cracked sidewalk. Thank you, tree.

Every morning, I light a candle and a stick of incense and I sit down on my cushion. I say, "I vow to be grateful for this precious human birth." I say, "I vow to be present. This is it."

The more I explore death, the more my life shines. The brightness of it. *Alive!*

Acknowledgments

An infinite number of causes and conditions made this book possible, which means that I am able to thank only a fraction of my benefactors.

Thanks to my supportive agent, Lindsay Graham, who helped me shape the initial manuscript, and to my editor at Shambhala Publications, Sarah Stanton, who invited me to submit a book in the first place. Sarah brought the perspective of a younger generation to her editing while connecting precisely to what I wish to say about old age and dying. Thanks to others on the editorial team at Shambhala for their skillful support, especially Audra Figgins and Emily Wichland. A deep bow to the friends and family who read parts of the book and gave me feedback: Louise Dunlap, Jaune Evans, Karl Goldstein, Fanny Howe, Katie Kahn, Peter Levitt, Kathleen Martin, Linda Norton, Bob Perelman, Henri Picciotto, Nora Ryerson, Cornelia St. John, Cynthia Schrager, Francie Shaw, and Mushin Terris. Some of these essays began as talks I gave, at the Everyday Zen Sangha and elsewhere, and I thank my dharma brothers and sisters and the sangha itself for providing a context for ongoing conversation about what really matters to us, and for joining me in these explorations of mortality. Two of these essays were first published in *Inquiring Mind*, and I offer special thanks to Barbara Gates, editor of that journal, for giving space to my work and for her editorial acuity. Thanks to the editors of *Tricycle*

Magazine for first publishing "Could I Be the Teacher They Expected?" originally titled, "The Old Woman of Pagazzano."

Some writers, not wanting to be distracted from their course, don't like to show their manuscripts until they are completed. I'm not that kind. I appreciate plenty of feedback along the way, and I received that gift from the other writers in my longtime writing group. This book would not exist without the thoughtful attention of Melody Chavis, Jenny Freeman, Barbara Gates, Linda Hess, and Christine Schoefer, who read and responded to these essays as I was working on them, sometimes patiently reading several drafts of the same essay. Thanks to Sandy de Lissovoy and Jeannie O'Connor for help with photography.

The major part of this book was written during the COVID-19 pandemic. I can't be grateful to a deadly virus, but I'm grateful for this year (and, oh dear, now it's more than a year) of writing and walking, masked or unmasked. I'm grateful for having a peaceful home that has sheltered me well during this time; grateful to my immediate neighborhood, where I have walked and walked and walked, except when the air was too smoky to go outside; grateful to the trees I have gotten to know, to my neighbors who have waved at me from their doorsteps, to Berkeley's Cesar Chavez Park, where I have walked by the water at all times of day, restoring myself in the company of scaups and coots. Most of all, I thank Francie and Bob, who never stop making our house a home and who have supported me in every way through this challenging time. My study is under the kitchen, and many is the time that one or the other of them has knocked on the kitchen floor with an upside-down broom, signaling that it's time for me to finish the sentence and come upstairs for dinner.

Permissions and Credits

Caplow, Zenshin Florence and Reigetsu Susan Moon, eds. "Asan's Rooster," "Ohashi Awakens in a Brothel," "The Old Woman's Enlightenment," "The Old Woman's Miraculous Powers," "Satsujo Weeps," and "Seven Wise Women in the Charnel Ground," in *The Hidden Lamp: Stories from Twenty-Five Centuries of Awakened Women.* Somerville, MA: Wisdom Publications, 2013.

Deshimaru, Taisen. "With Grandmother's Mind," in *Le Bol et le Baton: 120 Contes Zen.* Paris, France: Albin Michel, 1986.

Dogen. "Actualizing the Fundamental Point" (Genjokoan), "Instructions for the Tenzo" (Tenzo Kyokun), "On Nondependence of Mind," "The Time-Being" (Uji), and "Poems," in *Moon in a Dewdrop: Writings of Zen Master Dogen.* Translated by Kazuaki Tanahashi. New York, NY: North Point Press, 1985. Copyright © 1985 by the San Francisco Zen Center. Reprinted with permission of North Point Press, a division of Farrar, Straus and Giroux.

———. "Dharma for Taking Food" (Fushuku Hanpo), in *Dogen's Pure Standards for the Zen Community: A Translation of Eihei Shingi.* Translated by Taigen Daniel Leighton and Shohaku Okamura. New York, NY: SUNY Press, 1996.

———. "Old Dogen's Prayer" (Eihei Koso Hotsuganmon), in "Sound of the Stream, Shape of the Mountain" (Keisei Sanshoku), in *Treasury of the True Dharma Eye* (Shobogenzo). This prayer is chanted as a regular part of the Soto Zen liturgy.

———. "Only a Buddha and a Buddha," in *Treasury of the True Dharma Eye: Zen Master Dogen's* Shobo Genzo. Edited by Kazuaki Tanahashi. Boulder, CO: Shambhala Publications, 2012.

———. "Universal Recommendations for Zazen" (Fukanzazengi), in *Dogen's Extensive Record*. Translated by Taigen Dan Leighton and Shohaku Okamura. Somerville, MA: Wisdom Publications, 2004.

Fischer, Norman. *The World Could Be Otherwise: Imagination and the Bodhisattva Path*. Boulder, CO: Shambhala Publications, 2019.

Gore, Lesley. "It's My Party." By John Gluck, Wally Gold, Herbert Weiner, and Seymour Gottlieb. Recorded 1963. Track 3 on *I'll Cry if I Want To*. Mercury.

Hartman, Zenkei Blanche. *Seeds for a Boundless Life: Zen Teachings from the Heart*. Boulder, CO: Shambhala Publications, 2015.

The Heart Sutra: The Womb of Buddhas. Translated by Red Pine. Berkeley, CA: Counterpoint, 2009.

Hoffman, Yoel. *Japanese Death Poems: Written by Zen Monks and Haiku Poets on the Verge of Death*. Rutland, VT: Tuttle Publishing, 1986. Copyright © 1986 Charles E. Tuttle Publishing Co., Inc., reprinted with permission of the publisher.

Ryōkan. *One Robe, One Bowl: The Zen Poetry of Ryōkan*. Translated by John Stevens. Boulder, CO: Weatherhill, 1977. Reprinted by permission of Shambhala Publications.

Shantideva. *The Way of the Bodhisattva*. Translated by the Padmakara Translation Group. Boulder, CO: Shambhala Publications, 1997. Reprinted by permission of Shambhala Publications.

Wagoner, Porter. "A Satisfied Mind." By Red Hayes and Jack Rhodes. Recorded 1955. Track 1 on *A Satisfied Mind*. RCA Victor.

About the Author

SUSAN MOON is a writer and Buddhist teacher in the Soto Zen tradition. Her books include the memoir *This Is Getting Old*; the groundbreaking collection, *The Hidden Lamp: Stories from Twenty-Five Centuries of Awakened Women*, with Florence Caplow; and *What Is Zen?* with Norman Fischer. Susan is a contributor to *Lion's Roar*, *Tricycle*, and other publications. She lives in Berkeley, California, and practices at the Berkeley Zen Center and with the Everyday Zen Sangha. For many years she has taught and led Zen retreats in the United States and internationally. She hopes this is her last book about old age and death.